# GREAT STORIES
## OF THE
## GREAT LAKES

# GREAT STORIES
# OF THE
# GREAT LAKES

*by Dwight Boyer*

⚓

ILLUSTRATED WITH PHOTOGRAPHS
AND MAPS

FRESHWATER PRESS INC.
Cleveland, Ohio 44114

**Published  & Distributed by**
   **Freshwater Press, Inc.**
   **Cleveland, OH  44114**

Manufactured in the United States of America

*Library of Congress Cataloging in Publication Data*

Boyer, Dwight
   Great Stories of the Great Lakes     1966

         Includes Index.
         1. Great Lakes - History.   2. Shipping - Great Lakes - History
         I Title.
         F551.B7 1985  977  84-18790


   **ISBN 0-912514-49-3**

*To my father, Lawrence H. Boyer, who would have been supremely happy had he lived to see the fine grandson who now bears his name, this book is affectionately dedicated*

# Acknowledgments

A book of this nature, however modest, is seldom an individual effort. Rather, it comes into being largely because many people have given of their time and knowledge to uncover and make available those almost forgotten facets of history which, when assembled, supply the basis for a factual account of past events.

Their passion for accuracy and detail help the author bridge the pitfalls into which he might otherwise tumble. A sincere enthusiasm in matters related to the Great Lakes and their past dramas are, fortunately, the forte of such dedicated people as Janet Coe Sanborn of the Cleveland Public Library and the honored editor of *Inland Seas,* the quarterly publication of the Great Lakes Historical Society, of which she is also a vice-president. Help for a beleaguered author comes, too, from meticulous researchers such as Richard J. Wright, intensely devoted to the history of the Great Lakes and their ships, past and present; from Frank A. Myers and Richard F. Tappenden, who have devoted much time to chronicling the history of the Manitoulin Island area and an intensive investigation relative to the ancient wreck they believe to be the *Griffon;* from Walter and Teddy Remick, whose collection of Great Lakes material is seemingly unending; and from Beryl H. Scott, of Ft. William, Ontario, whose scholarly contributions to Canadian historical volumes have enlightened many of the present generation as to the fascinating early days along the north shore of Lake Superior.

Some of what might be called the "atmosphere" that inspired a continued interest in Great Lakes ships and the men, some long since departed, who sailed them was nurtured time and again by "yarning" sessions in darkened pilothouses while the author was on assignment for his newspaper. Willing and cooperative victims of endless questions were the late Captain W. Ross Maitland of the *George M. Humphrey,* Captain John H. Walton of the *James Watt,* Captain Sam Teigland of the tanker *Panoil,* the late Captain Clarence W. Fitch of the *Ralph H. Watson,* Captain Raymond Bissonette of the *Menihek Lake,* Captain John Johnson of the *Champlain,* Captain Richard R. Galbreath of the *Paul L. Tietjen* and Captain John P. German of the *Coast Guard Cutter Mackinaw.*

And then there were long evenings in the pilothouses of the Toledo tugs of the Great Lakes Towing Company, where, between tows, Captains Hugh Damas, Bill Bridge, Mike Tussay and the late Harvey Johnson were forever recalling events in which their skipper friends were involved. Often we were joined by the deck, fire hold and engine room boys. I remember Frank Shepler, Felix Knetschel and Freddie Keefer. Captains "Doc" Millard and "Dixie" Damas, both since departed, shared adventures together and passed along their experiences. Other Great Lakes Towing Company people who have been extremely helpful are Captain John Kelsner, Captain James Hallahan, Frank Fauver and Ross Mortimer.

Among other friends, afloat and ashore, whose encouragement and wise counsel was invaluable, are Captain Thomas F. Harbottle, Captain Henry F. Wiersch, Captain Wendell A. Parry, Captain M. S. Thompson, Captain Evor S. Kerr of the United States Coast Guard and Captain H. C. Inches, master mariner and curator of the Great Lakes Historical Society's Marine Museum in Vermilion, Ohio.

Help came too, from Don Spavin of the *St. Paul Sunday Pioneer-Press,* George M. Steinbrenner of Kinsman Marine Transit Company, Rev. Edward J. Dowling, S.J., of the University of Detroit, Bertram B. Lewis of the Lake Carriers' Association, George W. Callahan, retired vice-president of the Interlake Steamship Company and John C. Pallister of the American Museum of Natural History. My grateful thanks too, to artist Vince Matteucci of the *Cleveland Plain Dealer's* Sunday Magazine who gave generously of his time and rare talent.

And it goes without saying that without the patience of my wife, Virginia, who dutifully applied herself to her several hobbies while the author was occupied at the typewriter and thus provided uninterrupted hours of work, this book might never have been finished.

Inevitably, some have been forgotten. But their contributions will, nevertheless, always be appreciated.

DWIGHT BOYER

Mentor, Ohio

# Contents

# *Illustrations*

GREAT STORIES
OF THE
GREAT LAKES

# 1

⚓

# Tomorrow's Hero!

One brisk October afternoon in the year 1900, when owning a fast and commodious steamboat was not only more respectable but vastly more rewarding than guiding the reins of a two-minute pacing horse, a hopeful marine reporter for the *Detroit Free Press* was picking his way gingerly over the frayed hawsers that laced a Detroit River dock. On his right reared the red brick warehouse and general office of the White Star Line and on his left, where a score of roustabouts prepared her for winter layup, loomed the superstructure of White Star's new 308-foot luxury excursion steamer, the *Tashmoo*.

Of more immediate interest however, was the fact that dead ahead and quite by chance also loomed the bulk of Aaron A. Parker, White Star's president—a huge, brusque and standoffish former oil field "wildcatter" who had hit it big in Great Lakes shipping and whose office door was seldom open to casual reporters.

It also chanced that Parker, fresh from a heavy lunch and an eminently satisfactory session with his auditors, was in one of his mellower moods. Largely by virtue of the spanking new *Tashmoo,* just ending her first full season of service, White Star had enjoyed its most successful year.

"Quite a vessel you have here, Mr. Parker," ventured the reporter, with nothing more ambitious on his mind than a morsel for his column.

"Yes," rumbled Parker, a fragrant cigar in his teeth and one foot resting comfortably on a mooring bit, "she's a great ship. In still weather and on a straight course she can beat the *City of Erie* or the *City of Buffalo* with no trouble—no trouble at all!"

In substance, this was like challenging Dan Patch with an untried steed of doubtful lineage. The "city" boats were the pride of the Cleveland and Buffalo Transit Company—big, fast sidewheelers whose supremacy had never been questioned, or tested, for that matter, by any of the hundred or more passenger and excursion steamers on the lakes.

"That would be quite a feather in White Star's cap," grinned the reporter, adroitly keeping the conversation on course and away from shoal-water side issues, "the C. and B. people claim to have the fastest steamers afloat."

"Hogwash," roared Parker, waving his cigar toward the *Tashmoo*'s glistening pilothouse, "The *Tashmoo* is narrow, low and powerful—built like an arrow, while both C. and B. ships are wide as scows, draw too much water and have too much superstructure for real speed. Why, great balls of fire, man, I'd be willing to bet one thousand dollars she could show her sternpost to either of 'em!"

Indeed, rumors were afoot that the *Tashmoo* had made some secret test runs, but nothing could be documented by an authoritative source. Complaints had come to the *Free Press* that on her excursion runs up the Detroit and St. Clair rivers the ship had sent up such a bow wave that docks were temporarily inundated, small craft buffeted about and riverfront lawns washed out. To the reporter, these nuggets of information, coupled with Parker's boasts, spelled a story. Pounding away at his typewriter that night he wrote his account of Parker's challenge, little realizing that his few paragraphs would trigger off the greatest steamboat race on the lakes since the jousting of the *Natchez* and *Robert E. Lee* on the Mississippi in the 1870's!

In Cleveland next day, as drays were carrying away the *City of Erie's* overnight freight cargo, a highly agitated Thomas F. Newman, C. and B.'s general manager, nervously paced his office, pausing occasionally to snort indignantly and reread the *Free Press* story. After an hour or two of this he threw open his office window and yelled over to a deckhand polishing the *City of Erie's* brightwork:

"Get me Captain McAlpine and Mr. Rendall."

Captain McAlpine, it developed, was uptown on business, but five minutes later, preceded by a mustache the size of a clothesbrush, 250 pounds and six feet four inches of Scotch marine engineer answering to the name of James Yorsten Rendall was ushered into the office.

"Sit down and look at that," snarled Newman, grimly thrusting at him the paper and pointing out the offensive column.

Polishing his glasses with a bit of waste that chanced to be handy, Rendall read slowly, his progress slowed by intermittent mutterings, snorts and mild oaths.

"Blosh," he exploded, "why, dom it sir, the mon must be doft. I've heard mony's the waterfront fairy tale aboot the *Tashmoo,* but mark my words sir, she'll ne'r see the day she can stond up to the *City o' Erie* in a fair race!"

"I've heard she can do twenty knots," growled Newman, "maybe even twenty-one!"

"Fontostic," mumbled the engineer, alternately gnawing

his mustache and the brim of his uniform cap, "obsolutely and utterly fontostic!"

"Well, fantastic or not, I've got to make a decision," snapped the general manager. "Frankly, it's a bad business racing a freight and passenger ship against an excursion craft, but we've got a reputation for speed to maintain. Come now, Mr. Rendall, you engineering chaps have more tricks than a hound dog has fleas. Tell me honestly, do we have a chance?"

"Ah, me," sighed Rendall, "I dinna wish to lead ye astray, Muster Newman, but I doobt there's a ship on the lakes that can do twenty knots, includin' the *Tashmoo* and our ain vessel. As for the *City o' Erie* . . . weel, perhops eighteen knots would be reasonable under the richt conditions and a bit o' tinkerin' wi' her engines might gi' us a wee bit more. But fronkly, sir, I dinna trust that White Star crowd. They're a shifty lot, aye, a shifty lot."

"Well, by Judas, shifty or no, I'm going to call Parker's hand," roared Newman, thumping his desk lustily. "Meanwhile, Mr. Rendall, you'd best give some thought to that tinkering you were talking about!"

Summoning his secretary, Newman dictated a caustic reply to the challenge, directing it to the *Free Press* reporter.

Dear Sir:
My attention was attracted to your newspaper article having the heading, "Will Wager $1000" . . . Parker seemingly has been so prosperous that he is willing to give away $1000 . . . the equivalent of a gift. The only still water the *Tashmoo* would be on even terms with either of our vessels would be in dry dock . . . comparing the *Tashmoo* with them is much like comparing a 3-minute horse to the Abbott . . . However, men with the best of judgment sometimes err. . . . I enclose my personal check for $1000. . . . This is in acceptance of the offer to wager $1000 which Mr. Parker is reported to have made. . . .

Somewhat abashed at the results of his few moments of bragging but still adamant, Parker replied, reaffirming his belief in the *Tashmoo*'s superiority and enclosing his one-thousand-dollar check.

"This," wrote the delighted reporter, "begins to look like business."

During the next few weeks the terms and conditions of the race were thrashed out. The *City of Erie* was to represent the C. and B. line, the race to be run on Lake Erie over a ninety-four-mile course between the Cleveland harbor entrance and Erie, Pennsylvania. Seasonal bad weather precluded any meeting during the present season, the race date being established as June 4 the following spring.

Even while in the talking stage the coming race became virtually a contest between two cities that were natural rivals in any event. In 1900, before automobiles and good highways, a steamboat excursion was the highlight of the summer's activities. The *City of Erie,* although relatively a new boat, had built up a tremendous following throughout the entire midwest. And the spanking new *Tashmoo* had quickly won the hearts of Detroiters. On evenings and weekends she ferried hundreds of thousands to and from the resorts of Bob-Lo

Island, Fort Gratiot and Sand Beach. They dubbed her the *White Flyer*, or the *Glass Hack*, in tribute to the extensive use of glass to protect her passengers from the chill evening breezes.

But to neutral observers, and they were few, the race did indeed shape up as one between unequally matched horses, although, quite in reverse of Newman's boasting, it was the *City of Erie* that seemingly fell heir to the role of the three-minute horse.

Built only two years before the *Tashmoo* and in the same shipyard, the *City of Erie* was strictly a utilitarian vessel. She had a 44-foot beam, drew over 10 feet of water, was 324 feet long and in addition to a cavernous freight hold, had accommodations for six hundred overnight passengers. Licensed to carry 2700 on excursions, she required a complement of 108 officers and crewmen. The sleek *Tashmoo* was only 37½ feet of beam, had a draft of slightly over 8 feet and displaced slightly over half the tonnage of her rival. Strictly an excursion ship, she was unencumbered by freight holds and tons of ornate furniture that were featured in the *City of Erie's* many staterooms and lounges. Extreme breadth, over the side paddle wheels, was 77 feet for the *City of Erie*, 69 for the *Tashmoo*.

"Statistically," the reporter enlightened his readers, "there is great structural inequality, such as one might find in a contest between a sturdy, wide-bottomed skiff and a canoe!"

Even Cleveland, traditional center of the lakes shipping industry, was unprepared for the invasion of visitors who came to see the race. By May 30 all available hotel rooms had been booked. Late arrivals scanned the "rooms to let" columns in the local papers or took their chances in the loft barracks quickly established by shrewd operators of waterfront bistros. During the day they gathered in knots or jammed the halls and lobbies of the Perry–Payne and Western Reserve buildings, where almost every Great Lakes shipper maintained offices, bringing normal business routine nearly to a standstill.

The old *Cleveland Leader,* likening the event to the dramatic Mississippi River steamboat rivalries, commented: "For the first time in the history of the Great Lakes, officially, sentiment and a fierce pride in their respective vessels is overriding hard-headed business sense and practicality!"

Taking cognizance of what was seemingly shaping up as the greatest steamboat race of the new century, a writer from the staid old *St. Louis Post* spent a couple of days observing the excitement and wrote:

If this is provincialism, it is provincialism at its best. Seldom before have two metropolitan cities united heart and soul behind their entries. Cleveland is in a gay, expectant mood, its population swelled by hundreds, nay, thousands of strangers who do little but talk of the coming race, the entire body sometimes staying up all night to watch the *City of Erie* dock at her Cuyahoga River pier. Such an event has never yet occurred on the Great Lakes and doubtless will never occur again!

Both principals in the coming jousting, however, had long since resumed their seasonal chores, the *Tashmoo* embarking every morning and evening for the resorts, wide-eyed passengers crowding the companionways to peer into the engine room, where the big triple-inclined engines, a symphony in red and brass, hammered out a powerful and thrilling tune. The *City of Erie's* schedule called for the loading of freight and passengers at Buffalo late every afternoon, an overnight run to Cleveland, reversing the procedure the following night.

More than a million dollars has already been wagered [commented George Callahan, the *Cleveland Plain Dealer's* marine columnist]. This estimate I make from reliable reports of the betting among prominent shipping and allied industry men. How much more is actually riding on the outcome is unknown, but

it is an acknowledged fact that every waterfront saloon from
Duluth to Buffalo is openly making book on the race. And when
it comes to sailors betting in their favorite ship, the sky is the
limit.

So much money was in evidence, in fact, that Lew Mc-
Creary, manager of the Colonial Hotel, felt it necessary to
hire a special night guard to watch the hotel safe, where
$100,000 in betting money was stacked, $20,000 of it rumored to belong to Charles F. Bielman, one of White Star's
major stockholders. Bielman himself, oozing confidence, was
usually to be found in the Colonial's lobby, cigar glowing
and pockets bulging.

"Plenty of *Tashmoo* money here," he would taunt, "money
that says we'll make the '*City*' look like a garbage scow!"

At first violently against the test of speed, Bielman in recent
weeks had changed his attitude, and the about-face was a
source of worry to Newman.

"He's aware of something we don't know," he confided
gloomily to his secretary. "After all, they say the *Tashmoo*
has never run at top speed. Maybe it's as Mr. Rendall said—
they're a shifty crowd."

For the first time in their lives, the men who sailed the
two ships found themselves in the limelight. Skipper Hugh
McAlpine of the *City of Erie* and Captain Burt S. Baker of
the *Tashmoo* were both big, tough-talking masters, the kind
to demand respect of subordinates and enjoy the confidence
of passengers and stockholders. Neither, during the months
when the race developed from a thoughtless bit of bragging
to a major sporting event, had evinced any enthusiasm for the
contest, but both were the type to give their best and get the
most from the ships and crews, once the bargain was made.

"The *Tashmoo* had really never been run at full speed,"
Parker confided to his brother Byron. "When Baker opens
'er up the *City of Erie* will be lucky to stay in sight."

Aside from what seemed like a simple case of mismatching, the *City of Erie* was at another disadvantage. Unable to cancel her commitments, she took aboard her usual heavy freight cargo and 421 passengers at Buffalo on the afternoon of June 3. The *Tashmoo*, meanwhile, had been withdrawn from her run some days before and in drydock had been completely scraped and painted. Here, too, the *Tashmoo's* chief engineer Winfield Dubois directed by Arthur Matteson, designer of her engines, installed a six-inch bypass main steam line into the low-pressure receiver to increase the cylinder pressure.

"It'll probably not be necessary," grumbled Matteson, "but I'd rather have it and not need it than need it and not have it."

During the Buffalo layover, Rendall, who had indeed given much thought to the necessary tinkering, supervised his assistant engineers in inserting new piston ring springs in the *Erie's* high- and low-pressure cylinders and had himself slacked off all bearings to minimize friction and overheating.

"Aye," he grinned to George Turnbull, the first assistant, "she'll be a wee bit noisy but she'll noo overheat."

On a normal round trip the ship burned some eighty-eight tons of coal, but the supply delivered in Buffalo, instead of going directly into the bunkers, was piled along the freight-deck bulwarks. Rendall put second engineer Alex Milton in charge of a work party to hand-sort the entire load.

"We'll not be wanting any slate in the boilers tomorrow," he warned.

"No fear on that score, chief," assured Milton, nodding in the direction of the sorters, "like nearly every lad aboard, they've bet everything but the clothes they're wearing!"

Before the ship left the dock Rendall also had the ship's carpenter at work building a big, six-by-ten-foot wooden cofferdam around the condenser. In Cleveland, a huge load of cracked ice had been ordered for morning delivery. Sea water was normally used to cool the condenser and condense the exhaust steam. But the canny Scot had wisely anticipated overloading the condenser. By packing it in ice the lowered temperature would reduce the amount of circulating water needed, lessening the pump load and conserving all available power for propelling the ship.

Still not quite satisfied, he sought out McAlpine as the *City of Erie* cleared Buffalo piers.

"With the exception of the ice, she's as ready as she'll ever be," he confided. "But, t'will do noo harm to see what the old girl will do."

McAlpine, edgy and more than willing to settle the nagging doubts in his own mind, marked off a spot on the chart east of Erie. Taking a pair of dividers he held the other end at Cleveland's east pier breakwall light and did a bit of rapid calculating. It was an even hundred miles!

"When I ring down, give it to her," he growled, "I'd just as leave find out tonight if we're going to eat smoke tomorrow."

Abeam of the designated point, as the telegraph pointer jumped to "full ahead," Rendall eased the *City of Erie*'s throttles wide open for the first time in the life of the vessel. At normal cruising speed the 30½-foot paddle wheels made twenty-four turns per minute, but from the moment of the Captain's signal they lathered around at a fantastic thirty-two revolutions per minute, holding the pace steadily until off the east breakwall at Cleveland! As the slackened-off bearings caused the engines to pound somewhat, James Yorsten Rendall, feeling the cool bearing surfaces, sported the self-satisfied smile of a man who knows his business. Passengers aboard were totally unaware that they had just traveled the fastest one hundred miles ever made by a Great Lakes passenger ship on a scheduled run!

At the top of the engine room ladder the nervous McAlpine waited with the elapsed time figures, his bushy brows a question mark.

"Aye, she'll do," grinned the engineer, "she'll do."

"I don't know," grumbled McAlpine, "we found out what we can do, but from what I hear that Detroit boat runs that fast when she's checked down."

First aboard as the *City of Erie* made up to her river pier before dawn was Newman. Noting her early arrival, he suspected that his commander and chief engineer had enjoyed a private preview of the ship's capabilities and demanded the figures.

"Looks pretty good," he admitted, "but I'm worried—the *Tashmoo* came in looking mighty fast . . . mighty fast. And the crowd with her are as cocky as bantams."

The *Tashmoo* had indeed been impressive. Tugmen who had gone out to meet her reported that although she was obviously taking it easy, her power was so great that when she checked down to enter the harbor her stern actually bobbed up and down!

"A divil of a sight it was," expostulated harbormaster Pete Lynch, "Whoy, whin the tug took her line the skipper looked down and winked—jist as if to say, ye ain't seen anythin' yit, laddies!"

Oblivious of the attention she drew from those on the *City of Erie*, the *Tashmoo* was even then moored inside the lee of the breakwall, her lights burning brightly but no sign of unusual activity apparent.

"Oh," said Newman, almost as an afterthought, "forgot to tell you. We lost the coin toss for position and Captain Baker, of course, took the outside position."

"Damn," snarled McAlpine.

"Ah, weel," consoled his engineer, "dinna worry, sir, o' coorse the deeper water weel be a bit of an advontage but it willna lost long."

As soon as the passengers had debarked, McAlpine and Rendall had the third watch lower the big lifeboats into the shelter of the passenger deck bulwarks. Hundreds of chairs and benches were carried into the ornate dining salon. All but one of the ship's five flagpoles were lifted from their sockets and lashed to the topdeck. Both men wanted wind resistance reduced to a minimum—the ship's high and wide profile was enough of a handicap. As the sky changed from gray to pink the ice was shoveled into the condenser coffer-dam, the hand-sorted coal shoveled into the bunkers, the fires raked and the *City of Erie* settled down for a nap.

On the *Tashmoo*, meanwhile, supreme confidence reigned. Designer Matteson and engineer Dubois confided to Parker that the bypass steam line was really not necessary but had been installed as an extra safety factor for victory.

"It's in the bag," assured Dubois.

Parker must have concurred, for topside the *Tashmoo's* seven big lifeboats still hung in their davits and nine assorted flagpoles jutted into the air.

Strangely, however, Dubois made no provisions for condensing the extra steam the bypass line created automatically, generating back pressure and power loss!

Ashore, reporters from all over the nation were making final arrangements to wire stories back to their papers. The growing, aggressive *Cleveland Press* made some sort of journalistic history by assembling a staff of forty-two reporters and hired hands to cover the event. Crates of pigeons were trundled aboard the *City of Erie* to wing shoreward with bulletins. Reporters carried waterproof buoys to be tossed overboard at designated points where fast motor cruisers waited to pick them up. Bicycle speedsters waited on shore to rush the running account to telegraph stations. An elaborate system of ship-to-shore kite signals was set up in case the winged and water messengers failed. The *Press* was taking no chances on a slipup on the most important event in Great Lakes history!

In the editions of the morning *Plain Dealer,* weather forecaster Emmet Kenealy predicted "Fair weather for the race!"

At eight o'clock on the morning of the fourth, an armada of launches put out for the *Tashmoo,* while hacks and fancy carriages drew up to the *City of Erie*'s gangplank. Out of both launches and carriages climbed what probably constituted the most elegantly attired and prosperous crews ever shipped. By agreement, both ships were bound not to carry passengers, but by popular demand and mutual consent, hundreds of the nation's top industrialists and Detroit and Cleveland "bluebloods" were "signed on" as auxiliary deckhands and watchmen. With the army of phony hired hands and scores of newsmen aboard, both vessels appeared to the eye to have their usual complement of passengers.

Two of the *City of Erie*'s auxiliary watchmen were George H. Worthington, wholesale hardware magnate, and James Corrigan, who controlled a vast steel, shipping and iron ore empire. "Deckhand" Harvey D. Goulder, a prominent lakes attorney, joined the pair on the boat deck.

"I've got five thousand dollars riding on this ship," grumbled Goulder, nervously nodding toward the *Tashmoo.* "It seemed like a good bet at the time, but now I'm not so sure."

Like others, he had heard the rumor that the *Tashmoo*'s engines and boilers had been placed too far aft, making her, when under way, squat in a manner that caused her hull to "drag" water unnecessarily. Moored in the shelter of the breakwall, she showed no signs of the squat.

An estimated two hundred thousand people jammed the

municipal pier area, and thousands more could be seen on the roofs of downtown buildings as, promptly at nine o'clock, both ships, adorned by plumes of steam, moved slowly out of the harbor. Once outside the breakwall they turned west, circling to come abreast before reaching the starting line, marked by the steam tug *Lutz,* on which were the official judges.

Exactly at 9:37 a puff of white smoke burst upward from the cannon mounted on the bow of the tug, but the sound was muffled by the clamor that went up from shore. The great race was on!

Galvanized into action as their engine telegraphs clanged to "full ahead," engineers Dubois of the *Tashmoo* and Rendall of the *Erie* threw their throttles to maximum speed positions! The cheering and shouting were inaudible in the fireholds and scarcely noted by those in the pilothouses. Clustered around the starting line, hundreds of craft, from skiffs to excursion steamers, began to toss and bob in the heaving wake of the racers. Harbormaster Lynch had officiously kept the smaller craft at some distance, but even so several were swamped.

Rendall, now that the race had begun, relaxed somewhat. Making his rounds and feeling only cool bearings, he communed with his ship:

"Ah, noo, old girl, ye've got a chonce to show ye're stuff. Dinna fail us or ye'll make every mon aboard proctically a pauper."

Like the sailors in every port along the Great Lakes, the men of the *City of Erie* and the *Tashmoo* had bet everything but their undershirts on their ships.

To all appearances, a mile from the starting line the vessels were absolutely abreast; and at Euclid Beach Park, five miles from the starting line, the positions were relatively unchanged, although most of the twenty-five thousand spectators at the resort were of the opinion that the *Tashmoo* might have forged ahead by a few feet.

At Fairport Harbor, twenty-five miles east of Cleveland, where the two steamers would pass close to shore, a crowd of fifty thousand waited expectantly. All stores in the village had closed up shop; schools were dismissed for the day.

From here a fast motor launch brought the first bulletin to be flashed over the wire services:

*"City of Erie* falling behind!"

The deeper water of her outside position, giving her paddle wheels maximum "bite," had enabled the *Tashmoo* to build up a lead of two lengths. This situation began to change, however, once the shoal water was astern. Slowly, almost imperceptibly, the *City of Erie* narrowed the gap. At Ashtabula, another thirty miles to the east, the two ships, belching clouds of black smoke, were practically side by side!

Chewing morosely on a dead cigar in the shelter of the *Tashmoo's* bridge wing, Aaron A. Parker was prey to nagging doubts. Were the rumors of the ship's engines and boilers being placed too far aft being proven fact? A correctly designed ship moving at flank speed throws a high wave from each side, a wave that falls away and then subsides in the wake. The walls of water created by the swift *Tashmoo*, however, were drawn together by the suction of the ship's "squat," to explode in white water in her lathering wake! No doubt about it, the sullen Parker concluded, the rumors were true and being proven so before a nationwide audience!

"Damn it," he snarled savagely to Bielman, "we should have a mile lead right now."

Down below, Dubois and Matteson were now fully aware that failing to provide for the rapid condensing of steam in the high-pressure cylinders was likely to prove embarrassing. True, in ordinary conditions the mounting steam pressure could be ignored, but under the rules of the race a government boiler inspector had been assigned to each ship. And the cold-eyed gentleman aboard the *Tashmoo* would tolerate no tinkering with the safety valve, which had been "blowing off" at 175 pounds almost constantly since the start of the race.

Panicky, Dubois grabbed second engineer Robert Watts and screamed above the engine room din:

"Ice! Get me ice—all you can get!"

Bounding to the main deck, Watts collared a group of "auxiliaries."

"We need ice down below," he bellowed. "Get all you can find and as fast as you can get it!"

But it so chanced that the only ice aboard the *Tashmoo* was in the steward's cavernous ice chests, two or three hundred pounds, and another two hundred pounds in the cold-drink coolers. Quickly the available blocks were shoved to the engine room companionway; but in most cases the clumsy auxiliaries lost their grip, and the ice went tumbling down to shatter on the ladders or machinery. With nothing to contain the salvaged pieces, the ship's vibration made a mockery of Dubois' improvised cooling system.

In desperation, the engineer grabbed two of the auxiliaries, pulled a fire hose from its rack and motioned for them to play a stream on the condenser. The temperature of the incoming sea water was sixty-eight degrees, and it had little or no effect.

Aloft, it was apparent, too, that the ship's seven big lifeboats and numerous flagpoles were a tremendous disadvantage in the wind, which had begun to freshen.

"Damn the boats, it's too late for that, but get us some weight forward," stormed Baker. "I've already trimmed her as much as I can."

Wasting no time on formalities, first officer George Klinger commandeered another work party of twenty bluebloods.

Sweating like stevedores, the cream of Detroit's society circles hauled the *Tashmoo*'s two big grand pianos from the glittering dance lounge, jamming them far forward on the bow. Next came chairs, tables, benches, soft-drink chests and even spare engine parts. But the little added weight was not apparent in the ship's trim.

At Conneaut, where a great armada of pleasure craft waited, anchored well off course, another bulletin, wafted shoreward by carrier pigeon and rushed to the telegraph office, advised the waiting country that:

"*City of Erie* leads by a length!"

Indeed, from her starboard rail, crowded with auxiliaries and newsmen, it would seem that the *Tashmoo* was slowly but surely losing ground.

On the bridge, Parker, Bielman and Captain Baker ground their teeth, cursed and bemoaned their lack of preparation.

"Only a break can save us," moaned Parker.

But aboard the *City of Erie,* if they had but known, two situations were shaping up, one in the pilothouse, the other in the engine room, that could conceivably turn into the break they prayed for.

The *City of Erie* was propelled by a compound vertical-beam engine employing a Sickles cut-off valve gear. The steam intake valves that opened and closed in unison with the engine motion operated by a mechanical arrangement of valve lifters and dashpots. When working properly, the big intake valves snapped shut with little or no loss of steam. Off Conneaut, one of the valves began to malfunction. A defective spring was permitting a jet of precious steam to escape!

By a series of rapid calculations, based on an intimate knowledge of his engines, Rendall figured that it would take about 125 pounds of extra weight to get the valve operating at full efficiency.

Racing to the top of the engine room ladder, the big engineer grabbed the first man that passed. It chanced to be diminutive seaman Johnny Eaton, bound aloft with a pitcher of ice water for the pilothouse.

"Quick, mon," snapped Rendall, "what do ye weigh— what do ye weigh?"

"One hundred and twenty-five pounds," gasped the startled sailor.

Protesting violently, Johnny Eaton was tucked under the engineer's right arm, carried bodily down the ladder, handed a protective wad of wiping cloth, boosted to the top of the engine and his duty made clear.

"Up ye go, laddie," yelled Rendall over the tumult of the engine room, "ye're aboot to do ye're duty for ye're ship. Sit ye doon on that valve—and if ye've a mind to leave there's a muckle o' lads here who'll dom weel change ye're mind for ye!"

Looking down into a sea of unfriendly faces, the owners of which brandished such lethal objects as Stillson wrenches, Eaton decided to stay.

In the miles that followed, Eaton suffered the agonies of the damned. Clinging precariously to the valve's oily reciprocating rod and with only a few layers of cloth between his posterior and the sizzling hot valve top, Johnny Eaton was certain his nether regions were being fried to a turn.

Periodically then, came his anguished cries for "more rags."

"Gi' him a dosh of water," ordered Rendall.

Thereafter, at one-minute intervals, oiler William Riley was assigned the task of dousing Eaton with a pail of water, always directed where it would do the most good.

Beckoning Rendall to him, the suffering seaman yelled "how much farther?"

"Ah, noo, dinna worrit," consoled the engineer, cupping

his hands to make himself heard. " 'Tis only a few miles noo, and laddie—laddie, I've a hunch that tomorrow ye'll be a hero."

Hollow-eyed, soaking wet but steaming hot, Eaton could do little but croak piteously, "more water!"

Off Lake City, Pennsylvania, a few short miles west of Erie, retired skipper Captain Alton Anselman was viewing the distant vessels through his trusty telescope, a group of excited neighbors waiting for his observations.

"Let's see now," he mumbled, "the smoke is so thick it's hard to tell—yes, yes, that's the *City of Erie,* the one with the single stack—she's out in front by only a length and a half!"

Days before, McAlpine had chosen his best wheelsman, Ralph Brady, for the race, and aware that it takes a few minutes for a wheelsman to "get the feel" of a ship after the watch changes, had ordered Brady to stay on the wheel the entire trip. His relief, wheelsman Arman Smith, was standing by in a corner of the pilothouse, "just in case." And wheelsman Brady, taking his responsibilities seriously, had slept but fitfully since. Keyed up by the mounting excitement over the past few days, he was literally a bundle of compressed nerves, about to explode. All day, as the tension grew, Brady had clung grimly to the wheel, but now, with the finish line almost in sight, wheelsman Brady sighed and fell over in a dead faint!

Almost immediately the *City of Erie* yawed dangerously to starboard, the wheel spinning wildly!

Smith, who had removed his shoes to better get the feel of the pulsating ship, lunged at the whirling spokes as McAlpine and the first mate dragged Brady aside. Skillfully, Smith brought the ship once more back on its course, but brief as the incident had been, the *City of Erie* had lost most of its scant lead. The two ships were again almost abreast!

On the steamer *America,* anchored off Erie and marking

the official finish line, timekeepers John Donaldson and Captain Charles L. Hutchinson watched the two blobs of black smoke on the horizon—blobs that grew larger as the laboring contestants drew nearer. Safely anchored to the outside of the course, thousands of spectators watched from a dozen excursion steamers that had been chartered out of Buffalo, Detroit and Cleveland. Hundreds of small craft buzzed about, eager to see the finish but ready to dash to shelter on the lee side of the larger boats when the curling bow waves of the racers came surging shoreward. Excitement ran high!

When still three miles away and from the head-on perspective of the judges' boat it was still impossible to tell which ship was in the lead or, indeed, if either ship held any advantage! On they came, both surrounded by the clouds of smoke that came vomiting from their stacks to be borne ahead of them by now brisk but errant winds!

Crouched over the *America*'s bow centerpost and after flagpole, Donaldson and Hutchinson waited tensely, each with a signal pistol in his right hand, a stopwatch in his left.

Pistons hammering, bearings chattering and with Johnny Eaton still perched agonizingly on the sizzling valve, the *City of Erie* surged across the finish line, Hutchinson's pistol barked and the race was over!

Instantly a bedlam of whistles and bells saluted the winner, every craft on the scene honoring her with noise of one sort or another. Dozens of straw hats sailed outward from the winner's crowded decks, where millionaire auxiliaries and sooty, sweat-streaked firemen embraced each other and disported themselves like schoolboys. Even James Yorsten Rendall was in a mood to waste a little steam. The roar of Donaldson's pistol as the *Tashmoo* crossed the line was lost in a throaty, mocking blast from the *City of Erie*'s big whistle.

Both timekeepers compared their watches, nodded and beckoned the boatload of newsmen who waited expectantly.

"The *City of Erie* wins by forty-five seconds!" yelled Hutchinson.

Aboard the winner pandemonium still reigned. Surrounded by C. and B. officials, newsmen, auxiliaries and regular crewmen, Captain McAlpine modestly sought to escape the limelight.

"Here's the real hero," he yelled as Rendall approached the celebrants, "we did little but steer the ship—the race was won in the engine room and firehold. Come now, Mr. Rendall, speak up. Surely there were some dramatic incidents down in your own bailiwick, so to speak, and where, gentlemen—if you'll pardon me—it must have been hotter than the shades of hell!"

"Aye," nodded Rendall as the group hushed, "there was indeed some very dromotic droma doon below. Airly in the race the domned cronkpin on the starboard blower engine ran hot, cutting doon the droft to the furnaces and, notcherly, lowering our steam pressure. We had just aboot set it to richts when one of the springs on a valve lifter went bad."

In excruciating detail then, the towering engineer related the story of Johnny Eaton and his mad ride astraddle the burning hot valve cap, dramatizing his anguished cries and sufferings.

"But come," he thundered, "wi' all modesty and credit due every mon jock aboard, do ye follow me below, gentlemen, to pay homage to he who has gone far beyond the call of mere duty!"

Down they trooped to the still blistering floor plates of the engine room. A grinning fireman, sensing their mission, winked at Rendall and jerked his head toward the condenser. Here, inside the temporary cofferdam, only his feet and head protruding above what was left of the crushed ice, reclined Johnny Eaton. Pale and wan but feeling no immediate pain, possibly due to the bottle the engineer had thoughtfully provided, he smiled foolishly and shook the many proffered hands.

"Gentlemen," roared Rendall, "ye've just wutnessed the greatest steamboat race in the history o' the Great Lakes. And though ye may search near and far ye'll find no greater hero than the mon ye see here before ye—soothin' his wounds and slakin' his thirst!"

A rousing cheer went up, hands were shaken and once more the happy roisterers, scarcely able to breathe in the furnacelike engine room, wended their way topside.

"There," consoled the engineer, "did I noo tell ye that ye'd be tomorrow's hero. Why the papers will be full of it, laddie, full of it. Drink up, mon, drink up. Dinna ye ken the full impoct o' ye'r brave deed? Oh, there'll be a braw festival tonicht' wi' the lods spendin' their winnings, and while I suspect ye'll be thinking twice or maybe even thrice before ye sit doon to accept their plaudits, 'tis highly unlikely that ye'll have to pay for a single drink. So drink up, brave Muster Eaton, drink u—why, guidness gracious, I do believe the brave lad has passed oot!"

# 2

⚓

# *Bonanza at Skull Rock*

Just east of Catholic Point, where the gloomy bulk of the
Sleeping Giant sheltered them from the chill night winds
that whistled over Thunder Bay, the geological survey party
of Thomas Macfarlane made camp late one June afternoon
in 1868. Representing the Montreal Mining Company, they
had been exploring the mineral possibilities along the north
shore of Lake Superior since mid-May, visiting existing mines
near Jarvis Bay and always looking for evidence of silver and
copper "sign." From the campfire near where their Mackinaw
boat was drawn up on the beach, several small offshore islands were silhouetted as the sun sank down somewhere between Thunder Cape and Pie Island. One of them, about
three-quarters of a mile from the mainland, appeared to be
solid rock, roundish and singularly unimpressive.

"Looks like the top of a big skull sticking out of the water,"
muttered Gerald Brown, Macfarlane's assistant.

Indeed, in his very first rough working sketch of the shoreline and its several detached rocks and islands, Macfarlane
penciled in the name "Skull Rock" for lack of a better one.
It was at least descriptive.

What brought the party of seven to the rugged and inhospitable Ontario shore was a final peace between the Canadian authorities and some of the nation's mining companies. Much of Ontario was still largely unexplored, geologically, and, as time has since proved, was fantastically rich in a variety of minerals and precious metals. Meanwhile, across Lake Superior, the copper bonanza of Michigan's Keweenaw Peninsula was making history in eastern financial circles. Silver ore was also being found, and the tremendous scope of the high-grade iron ore deposits in Michigan, Wisconsin and Minnesota was just becoming apparent. There was every reason to believe, the Canadian mining firms maintained, that the same geological formations, characteristic of their own north shore, would yield similar treasures.

The catch was that the Crown reserved all rights to gold and silver discoveries. Unwilling to surrender what they logically figured to be theirs by right of exploration and development, most mining companies refrained from major investments in sites or production equipment.

For twenty-one years the Montreal Mining Company had been stubbornly holding to extensive Lake Superior claims they had acquired from the original claimant, Joseph Woods. The impasse had ended when the Crown reluctantly relinquished its reservations of gold and silver rights but instead established an annual tax of two cents an acre on mining claims.

One of Macfarlane's missions, beyond the discovery of economically productive mining sites, was to determine whether the Company's vast holdings warranted the two-cents-per-acre tax. The primary goal was the surveying of the "Woods Location," as it was called, roughly twenty-five miles east of Ft. William and The Station (now Port Arthur, Ontario).

Macfarlane pointed out to his men that while the area

they were exploring was rock composed of grayish flags and red and white sandstone lying in an almost horizontal position, it was not to be taken lightly even though such geological characteristics rarely yielded anything of value. The conglomerate beds of Keweenaw, he recalled, had originally been vastly undervalued by geologists who had never before observed valuable minerals occurring in horizontal stratas.

Skull Rock, Gerald Brown decided, was an ideal spot for one of the party's marker or picket stakes. Easily visible from the mainland, it would serve as a point from which true reference lines could be drawn. Early in July he and a couple of helpers rowed out to drive the picket stake. The "skull," he found, measured approximately 90 feet each way, with its rounded crest only 8 feet above the surface of Lake Superior. He observed, too, a fork-shaped mineral formation called *galena*. One "prong" lay across one side of the "skull," the other ran out under the water. Macfarlane, summoned from the mainland, quickly put three men to work blasting out some of the galena. On July 10 one of the party, John Morgan, found the first nuggets of metallic silver near the water's edge.

"Blast it," ordered Macfarlane.

A single charge detached all the ore-bearing galena above the water line. But farther out large patches of the greenish rock could be seen. Morgan led the charge. Teeth chattering from the frigid inland sea, they fished up many of the loose rocks. The galena, they found, was intermixed with spots of an oxidized black mineral, heavily tinged with green.

With a little borax and what he called his "blowpipe," apparently a portable forced-draft charcoal torch, Macfarlane reduced the substance to metallic silver, exposing immediately the extraordinary richness of the black portions of the vein.

In the light of the campfire that night, he erased "Skull

Rock" from his rough map, renaming the rock "Silver Islet."

The next day the men continued to work up to their waists in the numbing water. Using crowbars, they pried up many more large hunks from the exposed vein. In all they recovered 1336 pounds of high-grade ore that, five days later, packed in a huge barrel, was shipped from Ft. William down the lakes to Montreal.

History has perhaps distorted the value of that first sample from Silver Islet, but the figure of $10,000 appears consistently. In any event, it was the most startling mineral discovery to date in Canadian geological history.

With the first warm weather of 1869 a shaft was begun practically at the water's edge, where the rich vein began its downward slant. It was the Montreal Mining Company's initial step in converting the Silver Islet site into a working, productive mine. Yet, from the very beginning it was evident that they would have to fight Lake Superior for every ounce of silver they recovered. Exposed to miles of open water in every direction but from the immediate north, even mild storms sent waves booming over the highest point of the islet. A sturdy house was built over the shaft and just as quickly was battered to bits. Rebuilt, it was then protected by a heavy timber shield. Still the seas found their way into the shaft, and when the lake was calm several small "feeders" inundated the workings. Operations were temporarily suspended.

During the winter of 1869–1870 several men stayed on at what the Company still called its Woods Location. When the island was frozen in they cut holes in the ice, planted explosive charges and blasted the vein, easily visible in the clear, cold water. When the shattered ice froze again—and it didn't take long—they cut more holes and with crude, long-handled claw-tongs lifted out the loosened ore. During that long winter, when the temperature often dipped to forty degrees below zero, working in Arctic conditions, they brought up well over eight tons of ore. This is not an impressive figure, but it was probably the richest silver ore ever unearthed on the North American continent. And when the timbered shores of nearby Burnt Island and Catholic Point echoed the hooting of the first steamboat whistle in May, the ore was sent on its way to Montreal.

Thomas Macfarlane had warned his superiors that it would take $50,000 to build a producing mine on Silver Islet. This figure later proved to be only one twenty-fourth of the actual cost, but in 1870, $50,000 was a fortune not to be risked without a soul-searching review by the decision-makers in Montreal. They were prepared to burrow through mountains, alter the landscape of a continent or build roads to distant claims of promise. But putting hard money into the future of a mine on a rock that was exposed to and repeatedly battered by great storms was another matter. They were realists, these men in the front office, and they knew Lake Superior. In the end, although they had already made $23,115 on a mine that was scarcely started, they decided to sell all their holdings in the area and take their profit.

When they found no prospective purchasers in Canada, word of the availability of the property was diplomatically made known in British financial circles. But speculative money was no easier to promote in England. A couple of overseas capitalists nibbled cautiously at the bait but later backed off. Canada was far away, its mineral possibilities still largely in the rumor stage and mining was still the chanciest of investments.

Down in Detroit, however, industrialist Alexander Sibley knew a promising deal when the elementary facts were made known and the primary problem revealed, even though the venture admittedly involved more than an element of gamble. In a short time he organized a syndicate to buy the Woods Location and formed a company to mine the Silver Islet site. The purchase price was $225,000.

Having made himself a bargain, Sibley set about to make it pay off. And the best way he could think of to bring about that happy situation was to appoint William Bell Frue as superintendent.

Few men have ever faced the challenge thrown at Frue, but for that matter, even fewer have had such an opportunity to share in the profits. A stockholder in the new company (he held 100 shares out of a total of 1600) his annual salary of $5000 was equal to that of Sibley, the president. Moreover, he had the promise of a bonus of $25,000 if, within one year, the net proceeds of the mine should suffice to repay the investors their purchase price of the property.

Frue was a realist, too, and knew that he had the world's largest body of fresh water to tame before the mine could be counted on to yield a steady, day-by-day return. A mild-mannered man of forty, he was a meticulous planner who, having armed himself with the ammunition he thought necessary for the conflict, went at his task with the bulldog determination of one who would brook no verdict but victory.

At Houghton, Michigan, he chartered the steamer *City of Detroit* to carry his working party of thirty-four men and the needed supplies to Silver Islet. Hoisting engines, boilers, pumps, cables, lumber, nails and tools—all the material to establish a self-subsistent community were stowed in the steamer's holds or lashed to its decks. And when she left the dock at Houghton the *City of Detroit* also towed a big scow with more heavy machinery and a raft composed of 20,000 feet of heavy square timbers. This was to become Frue's first line of defense against Lake Superior.

On September first, having enjoyed one of the lake's benign moods during the crossing, the steamer and its scow and raft tied up at the little wharf the Montreal Mining Company had built on the mainland. It was known as Silver Islet Landing, referred to today simply as the Landing. A pleasant pine grove within a stone's throw of the wharf was to be the site of a village to house the families of supervisory workers. Barracks-type structures or boardinghouse quarters would care for the miners. The little community was to be ready to shelter them through that first hard winter.

Throughout September Frue and his men worked up to eighteen hours a day constructing a breakwater made up of 460 feet of standing cribbing, bolted together with iron rods two inches in diameter. Behind it they filled in with rock and heavy rubble from the mainland shore. Help was short, so the officials and foremen worked along with the miners, timbermen, engine operators and laborers. Another crew was busy building a cofferdam that enclosed 70 feet of the vein. The breakwater was designed specifically for protection from the great storms that came hammering in from the southeast. This was the first enlargement of Silver Islet.

Mining operations actually got underway on October 5 and proceeded apace for three weeks before Lake Superior took note of the upstarts who would wrest the treasure from her bosom. A heavy southeast storm built up seas that in a couple of hours demolished 200 feet of the new breakwater, holed the cofferdam and filled the shaft with rubble the waves brought in with them.

Frue, examining the wreckage when the tempest had subsided, took particular note of twisted and bent lengths of the two-inch iron rods that had once held the big timbers together.

"One of my wife's hairpins would have done as much good," he observed to Charles H. Palmer, the project's chief engineer.

Never one to cry over what was already done, Frue set about building a bigger and better breakwater. By adding more cribbing and hauling in hundreds of tons of rubble he extended the base to a width of 26 feet. Despite the time lost in the bouts with Lake Superior, the last ship of the season after unloading its coal cargo steamed away from Silver Islet with a load of ore valued at $108,000.

The smoke of the departing steamer had scarcely been dissipated by the wind when another autumn storm swept the lake. Again giant seas, building up for nearly two hundred miles, assaulted the little island. The breakwater was once more pounded into matchwood, permitting thousands of tons of rock fill to slide down into deep water. And of the 20,000 feet of squared timber towed across the lake from Houghton, scarcely a single stick survived. Quickly, organized working parties set out to cut and drag timbers from the mainland forests. From these hastily hewn trees a still stronger and larger barricade was built. Mining operations again got underway.

Frue had not really underestimated the power of Lake Superior, but he had not counted on the time and extra effort of the entire party in repairing its ravages. He had planned on having a fairly substantial village ready for late October occupancy. But the weary men, sometimes working by the light of lanterns, had been able to erect only one large log structure.

At Houghton, meanwhile, the invasion force of families was gathering. Already burdened with additional mining machinery Frue had ordered, the old sidewheel steamer *Algoma*, Captain Simms, master, took aboard a considerable number of women and children, along with household furniture, family heirlooms, trunks and food supplies that, hopefully, would carry the colony through the winter.

The *Algoma* was a slow, plodding old craft, and by the time her lines were cast off on the afternoon of November 3, she was down to her marks. Many hopes and fortunes were in the hands of Captain Simms as he rang down for steam. Already upper Michigan was deep in snow. Small streams were frozen over, and the harbor was rimmed with ice. All went well while the *Algoma* was still sheltered by Keweenaw Point, but once out in Lake Superior it was a different story. They were hit almost immediately by a heavy northwest gale that intensified during the night. Blinding snow reduced visibility to a few feet; the spray froze on the decks and the old steamer rolled and pitched villainously. Down below all the passengers were terrified and deathly seasick, all convinced that they would never see another dawn. It was only one hundred and fifty miles to Silver Islet, but it took the creaking and groaning old *Algoma,* laboring all the time in head seas, two long days and nights to make it. Not even the disheartening sight of a single building to house them could quiet the cries of thankfulness given out by the passengers when they disembarked on the desolate coast on November 6.

Most of the women and children were bunked in the big log building while a village of tents sprang up to house the men. And this in country where the snow builds up to five feet and the temperature often drops to forty degrees below zero! The women's house left much to be desired. The logs were green, sweated when the stoves were fired up and were forever shrinking. During the nights, when the fires went out, the piercing cold built up deposits of hoarfrost. It was decidedly unpleasant.

Long before relief could be expected the food situation grew serious. Fortunately, the men helped vary the menu and stretch the supplies by chopping holes in the ice through which the fishermen in the group were able to draw up huge lake trout. Every morning during that long winter the men trudged out over the ice to the mine while the women thawed out moss to stuff between the rows of shrinking logs. Despite what would today be considered almost unendurable hardships, Dr. Tompkins, the community's surgeon-in-residence, was able to report that the winter passed without a single casualty.

The spring of 1871 brought several storms. The first one, in March, featured huge chunks of ice, borne at express-train speed by mountainous waves. These had the effect of massive battering rams. The men fled the mine site but even on the mainland, three-quarters of a mile away, they could hear the cracking, rending and booming as the ice sheets reared over the breakwater and were driven on by the relentless pressure of more ice and the persistent seas. Altogether, Frue estimated that the spring gales of '71 cost him 50,000 feet of timber, many tons of iron bolts and 6000 tons of rock fill. The mine was in a shambles. But once more Frue built a bigger breakwater; this one, with a base of 75 feet, rose 18 feet above the lake and was bolstered by stone from the mine itself.

Home construction ashore went on briskly and, in spite of time spent in repairing storm damage, the miners recovered $1,000,000 in silver ore.

Frue had won his $25,000 bonus.

By 1872, when the company issued its first report—and long overdue it was, some thought—it noted that there had been great changes along the once lonely and desolate shore.

They have transformed it into a thriving and industrious settlement with a church, schoolhouse, store, custom house, post office and substantial dwellings for over 500 men [the report went on]. They have made it the best harbor of refuge on the northern shore of the lake, with a lighthouse on Silver Islet and range lights on the mainland. There are extensive wharfs for shipping ores and supplies, with basins protected by breakwaters . . . with three steam tugs and a sectional dock for repairing vessels. Silver Islet itself has now been enlarged to over two acres, well protected against storm and water, and covered with buildings for the mining, assorting and packing of the ore. This mine is without question the most remarkable silver mine in the world.

But for those who labored to wrest her treasure, *trouble* was synonymous with the name Silver Islet. The year of 1873 made a promising beginning, but before it was half over the vein of silver, on which so many depended, almost ceased to produce. But the vein had constantly been shrinking and then widening out again. They dug on.

Down in the shaft the miners had encountered nothing more than an ordinary and expected quantity of water or seepage. But on October 24 they struck a "feeder," which at once drove them from the bottom of the mine, the water rising about 10 feet per hour. The mine was supplied with five- and six-inch draw-lifts, and although an eight-inch plunger pump was in reserve at the surface, Frue at once dispatched a tug to Houghton to telegraph Detroit for a twelve-inch plunger pump. This was completed and shipped on November 14, but the steamer carrying it became frozen in at Houghton.

While the miners were fighting their battle with the rising water in the shaft, Lake Superior was girding her loins for another blow at the interlopers. A heavy storm from the southeast hit near the middle of November, followed by a real "gagger" on the first of December. This one tore away 350 feet of submerged cribbing and caused a loss of 20,000 feet of timber, 7½ tons of bolts and 5000 tons of rock. The major breach was in the center of the main breakwater, which now had a height of 20 feet. John Gilbert's blacksmith shop, which stood inside the breakwater and about 50 feet from it, simply disappeared. The tremendous upsurge of the seas lifted the lost stones of former fills and hurled them around the islet like giant hailstones. While the tumult raged the miners kept steam up and the pumps running to hold the flooding in check. They did not fully succeed until January 8, when another eight-inch plunger was fitted in. From that day on the water was easily controlled.

However, as the mining went on the rate of the inflowing water increased, finally leveling off at 155 gallons per minute. Another pump was installed, and the combination of pumps kept the shaft reasonably free of water. But they had to be kept running 24 hours a day, 365 days a year. They became as much a part of Silver Islet as the rock itself, and after a time even the most recent arrivals among the miners became less and less conscious of the noise.

The mine ultimately reached a depth of 1230 feet. Fifteen levels, or tunnels, intersected the main shaft, and most of these were 200 feet or more in length. The ninth level went far beyond the others, measuring approximately 1360 feet. Furthermore, most of the levels had cross-cuts (more tunnels) running out at right angles. A vertical shaft went down to the ninth level, an inclined shaft was sunk to the full depth.

Frue had personnel problems that would not have been inherent to a conventional mining operation. The men whose families were comfortably housed on the mainland were dependable. But many in the barracks and boardinghouses on the islet itself were, by nature, drifters, ready game for the peddlers of bad whisky who were always nearby. When off duty they were inclined to take unauthorized vacations or indulge in prolonged drinking bouts ashore. A library, established on the islet, had little appeal. Prospective recruits arrived by steamer, took one look at the place they were supposed to work and hastily climbed back aboard. Frue eventually obtained a liquor license for the mining company and installed a bar in one of the boardinghouses. From then on liquor was rationed, with extra portions for good behavior.

For all the troubles on the islet, life on the mainland was apparently quite delightful. Company officials often spent their summers in houses built for them, and the homes of those in responsible, year-around positions on the mine project were comfortable and well furnished. There were musical evenings, dances, literary sessions, boating, picnics and beach dinners. The company tug, *Silver Spray,* was much in demand for moonlight cruises during the summer and for taking guests out to the fishing grounds, where big lake trout were found in great numbers. Over on the islet a brass band was organized, and on warm nights the mainlanders often lounged on the dock or on their porches while stirring, if imperfect, renditions drowned out the throbbing of the pumps. There were happy times as well as difficult ones for those associated with Silver Islet.

By now the true character of the mine had shown itself, although the fact was not bandied about beyond the official circle. The major vein had a habit of contracting almost to the point of disappearing. And then, when the silver yield seemed about to end forever, it would widen out to 20 feet or more. So the mine followed a pattern of good times and bad. The best of the good times were two real bonanzas, struck four years apart.

It was shortly after the first when Frue resigned, giving no reason (at least to his close associates) but merely expressing his regrets. Some thought the extreme efforts over the years had been too much, that his health was beginning to falter. More likely, others said, it was his invention and the necessity of spending more time perfecting it. The Frue Vanner (an ore separator) was developed in a workshop built on the bank of a small mainland stream. The vanner was so great an improvement on existing types that it later became standard stamping-mill equipment all over the world.

It is possible that without him Silver Islet would never have been anything more than what Thomas Macfarlane first saw—a skull-shaped island of rock. But in any event, on the first of August, 1875, William Bell Frue walked away from it, boarded a steamer at the Landing and sailed away over the lake he had bested through sheer guts and determination.

Before the second bonanza was struck, in 1878, the mine had almost petered out. The company was heavily in debt. Frue's method had been to mine in levels, leaving a substantial "roof" between levels, the roofs being supported by pillars of rock ore left standing. Competent geologists estimated that some of the standing pillars in the most productive levels contained $10,000 in ore. Others held that the large bodies of rich ore in the roofs themselves were worth anywhere from $350,000 to $500,000. Several schemes for the removal of the ore after constructing artificial roofs were discussed. Fortunately for all concerned, several small strikes of good ore were made and, for the time being, the hazardous artificial-roof ideas remained as such.

The first bonanza was accepted as a matter of course and a "we knew it was there all the time" attitude. The second was the subject of great joy down in the mine and at the landing and great hosannas of relief at the head office.

One of the engineers connected officially with the mine described the appearance of the second bonanza as

An inverted cone with a base of about fifty feet on the third level with the apex down as far as the fifth level. This deposit was phenomenal in its structure. A winze [a small shaft sunk from one level to another, usually for ventilation] in the middle of the deposit to the fourth level, sixty feet, was sunk literally through native silver, the metal standing out boldly from the four walls of the winze!

Everybody connected with the project knew that, if necessary, the mine could operate without a full crew of "deep" men, or hard-rock miners, or even with a vastly reduced supervisory force. But there was one commodity without which it could not function, even for an hour. Coal had been the lifeblood of Silver Islet since the beginning of operations—coal dug in faraway Ohio and hauled by steamer to the islet. Without it the boilers could not produce steam for the hoists, crushers or sorting mills. More importantly, without it the pumps would inevitably thump to a stop.

Coal arrived at regular intervals throughout the season, a considerable surplus being maintained. Each November, just before navigation closed, the last coal boat would bring another thousand tons that, with that already on hand, constituted the winter's supply. And since the great enlargement of the original site, it was stored where the searching seas of Lake Superior would be unlikely to reach it.

Actually, it was a shortage of coal, coming on the heels of the bad times that followed the second bonanza, that closed the mine.

There are several stories of why the steamer and its vital coal cargo failed to reach Silver Islet. One version has it that the vessel put into Houghton for minor repairs only to be frozen in before the work could be done. Another story is that the crew indulged in a week-long engagement with Demon Rum, during which time the ship became ice-bound. Still another yarn advances the theory that the crew, attracted by the high wages prevailing in the nearby lumber camps, decided to spend the winter in the woods and that the freeze-up came before the harassed skipper could muster enough experienced seamen to risk the trip to Silver Islet. It may have been a combination of all the rumored circumstances, or none of them. The important thing was that the steamer was still at Houghton when the December weather, unusually severe that year, ended any possibility of completing its scheduled trip.

On January 20, 1884, Frue's successor, Richard Trethewey, wrote to the head office:

Ere long we shall find ourselves placed in a serious dilemma owing to the non-arrival of our winter supply of coal last fall. . . . a vessel with nearly one thousand tons having failed to reach here, being laid up en route. The present supply of coal is sufficient to run with until about the first of March, after which we shall find it extremely difficult to carry on the work.

For all the talk of silver, timber, iron bolts, rock fill, liquor, food, housing, libraries and brass bands, it was coal that kept Silver Islet in business.

Trethewey was right. In March the fires died out, the pumps wheezed to a stop and then, quite rapidly, Lake Superior took the shaft once more into her embrace. Now, when the great storms pounded holes in the breakwater and flung boulders through the buildings, the damage went unrepaired. Silver Islet could not fight back. But in the years the waters of the lake were stayed, the shaft and its working levels had yielded a fabulous $3,500,000 in silver.

Later that spring, when navigation opened, a general exodus began and continued until only the Cross family was left. For nearly half a century Captain Cross took care of the abandoned Silver Islet Mine and the Landing structures associated with it. His name became synonymous with Silver Islet, and proof of his vigilance lay in the fact that, except for moss and normal deterioration, all the buildings on the islet and mainland remained much the same for many years.

There were rumors, unconfirmed but repeated through the years, that the mine geologists had some basis for thinking there was another rich vein, one that lay almost parallel to the original one. And it was known fact that the ore in the pillars and roofs was the same grade that had made the mine one of the richest in history. It was perhaps the possibility of harvesting both that inspired a Duluth firm to take an option on Silver Islet in 1920. They dewatered part of the old workings for exploratory purposes but apparently failed to find the rumored vein, for they soon abandoned the search. The operation is said to have cost $84,000 while returning only $10,971.97 in silver.

About the turn of the century families from Ft. William and Port Arthur began using the cottages in the deserted village for summer homes, as others do to this day. The "Island," they call it, a misleading name by which the old Landing is now known. For years it was accessible only by Lake Superior in summer, by snowshoes or dog teams in the winter. Now a good highway leads to the door of the old mining company general store that, unaltered, still serves the cottagers. The massive old iron safe that once guarded the miners' savings is still in place. The bar sports the initials of many who knew Silver Islet in its balmiest days. A historical marker near the store enlightens the casual visitor as to the drama unfolded there long ago. Some of the log houses still stand and are used, including that of Captain Marin, who operated one of the mining company's tugboats.

And out there, offshore, is Silver Islet. Nothing remains of the buildings or equipment. Lake Superior and the ravages of time have claimed nearly every physical evidence of the history enacted on that tiny bit of rock. Silver Islet itself, because of its flooded shafts, is off limits. A few trees make a brave attempt to achieve stature, even as did the breakwaters of William Bell Frue, but with considerably more success.

Other than that, Silver Islet, if one ignores those dark and ominous water-filled shafts, looks much as it must have when Gerald Brown muttered to Thomas Macfarlane . . . "Looks like the top of a big skull sticking out of the water."

# 3

⚓

# Johnny Green's Date with Destiny

Johnny Green had a date with destiny on the ghostly hulk of
a tragic ship lying in the dark depths off Long Point—one
deck down, three windows aft the wheelhouse!

Here, off the long sandy hook of land that sweeps down
from the Canadian mainland of Lake Erie, lie the ribs and
plates of scores of ships and the bones of hundreds of sailors.
Rarely has the temptation of riches on a single sunken vessel
so obsessed a man that he risked his life for it, not once, but
many times. And like the moth who flits to the lamp once
too often, the last trip nearly finished him. But if he were
alive today, Johnny Green would probably still be prowling
along the bottom of Lake Erie . . . searching . . . searching . . .
searching . . . one deck down, three windows aft the wheelhouse!

The object of Johnny's insatiable quest was in the *Atlantic*,
a fine, big side-wheel passenger and freight ship whose ex-
cellent performances on the Buffalo–Detroit run had earned
her the reputation of being a comfortable and speedy vessel.
Over the years the *Atlantic* and Johnny Green became so in-

separably entwined in the lore of the Great Lakes that to mention one without the other would be an injustice to both.

We begin, then, with Johnny Green, the farm boy from Ogdensburg, New York, an energetic youngster who first learned to swim in the cold waters of the St. Lawrence River. Later, when his father bought a farm near Oswego, he continued to swim daily from early spring to late fall, this time in Lake Ontario and Oswego harbor. A great natural swimmer, he had the rare ability to hold his breath for long periods underwater. This skill came to light at the age of fifteen, when he successfully recovered stolen articles from fifty feet of water off the Oswego dock. From then on, when property or valuables were lost overboard anywhere in the vicinity, the call went out for Johnny Green ". . . that young fellow who can stay underwater so long." He recovered bodies, anchors, lost freight, anything of value. In a single summer he brought up sixteen tons of pig lead, sixty tons of railroad iron and, from the wreck of a British gunboat lost during the war of 1812, cannon, swords, cannonballs, muskets and other implements of war. By the fall of 1841 he was already familiar with the bottom of Oswego River, the harbor and adjoining areas of Lake Ontario. Sale of the salvaged items proved profitable; but the diving season was short, and the long winters he spent working in a machine shop. After eleven summers of diving the young man's bankroll totaled $11,000, and in the spring of 1852 he, his brother and some of his brothers-in-law booked passage on the propeller *Oswego,* all determined to build new lives for themselves in the West. The *Oswego* passed through the Welland Canal early one morning and was steaming peacefully down Lake Erie, off Cleveland, when Green retired for the night. Shortly after midnight the *Oswego* was rammed by the steamer *America* and went to the bottom in less than five minutes, carrying down four of Green's party and scores of others. The sur-

vivors were still being pulled aboard the *America* when Johnny Green began to dive for people entangled in the wreckage of the *Oswego*. Once he stayed down so long that when he surfaced blood gushed from his mouth, eyes and ears. Half-conscious, he was dragged aboard the *America* and, with the other survivors, rushed to Cleveland.

Although practically penniless and with nothing but the clothes he stood in, Green camped on the shore for two weeks until the bodies of his friends had come ashore and had been decently interred. His trunk and those of other passengers came ashore, too, but they had been stripped of money and valuables by vandals.

Fate plays strange tricks, and here, as he searched for the disaster victims, the future course and years of Johnny Green were shaped. Nearby and a short distance offshore, he witnessed his first scientific diving expedition, where men in regulation armor were exploring the wreck of the steamer *G. P. Griffiths,* sunk two years earlier just west of Fairport Harbor. The divers were reluctant to let Green try their gear until he jumped over the side of the wrecking schooner and stayed under for nearly three minutes! This convinced the gentlemen that Green knew something about diving, and before the day was another hour older he went down on the wreck in one of their armored suits and stayed thirty minutes, longer than the experienced divers.

Completely fascinated by the new worlds opened to him with protective gear and an air supply, Green at once determined to spend the rest of his life as a commercial diver. He joined the loosely knit salvage organization and proposed that they attempt to get some of the wealth from the *City of Erie,* another passenger ship that had burned and sunk in deep water with a rumored $50,000 in gold, most of it the life savings of the immigrants she had been carrying.

The wreck lay in 71 feet of water, and although his companions expressed the fear that a man could not work at that depth without being crushed to death, Green proved them wrong by successfully recovering quite a sum of money. Later, although others said it could not be done, he actually raised the burned-out hulk and towed it to shore.

But while Johnny Green was prowling the hull of the *City of Erie,* a tragedy that was to make a certain lost safe the passion of his life was taking place on Lake Erie, this time off Long Point.

The *Atlantic,* back on her Detroit–Buffalo course after a stop at Erie, Pennsylvania, was steaming slowly through a heavy fog in the dark early-morning hours of August 19, 1852. Pacing the wheelhouse sleeplessly as the ship's bell tolled out warning clangs at regular intervals, Captain J. Byron Pettey was grumbling to the wheelsman about the vessel's overcrowded condition. There had been more than the normal complement of passengers at Detroit, about three hundred in all, and a great tonnage of freight. Despite this, the *Atlantic* was committed to stop at Erie to pick up two hundred Norwegian immigrants, bound for Quebec. But the Captain had been obliged to leave seventy-five of them on the wharf— there just wasn't room for them. As it was, those taken aboard were bedded down on the hurricane deck, on the forepeak and in the companionways. Their trunks, boxes and bundles —their sole wordly possessions—were piled all over the ship. Adding to the Captain's worries was $36,000 in American Express Company gold, reposing in the purser's safe.

"I'll be damned glad," he confided to first mate Howard Harmon, "when we get to Buffalo and get rid of that money and the Norwegians."

Suddenly there was a frightened, fog-distorted cry from the bow lookout: "Steamer off the port bow!"

There was a flurry of shouted orders, a hasty clamoring of steam whistles, a great clanking of metal as the ship's big walking-beam engine thrashed violently astern and finally, a hollow rumbling as the *Atlantic* was rammed forward of the port wheel by the propeller steamer *Ogdensburg!*

Like two dogs that have tangled viciously but briefly and then backed off to survey the damage wrought, the ships drifted apart after the collision, neither, apparently, seriously holed. But minutes later a begrimed and frightened fireman sought out the Captain to report that the *Atlantic* was flooding below with water spurting up through the engine-room gratings. Shortly the vessel began to settle. Captain Pettey gave the "abandon ship" order and the crew began their orderly routine of lowering boats and assigning seats. But the terrified Norwegians, who understood no English, panicked at the shouted orders and began to jump overboard. By now the water had reached the fires and huge clouds of steam began spurting up from the skylights and companionways. In this eerie scene of disaster the *Atlantic* made her final plunge, leaving the surface of the lake cluttered with wreckage, trunks and drowning passengers. On the *Ogdensburg,* which had come to a stop a mile away while her crew made temporary repairs to her stove-in bow, the captain heard the frenzied screams from out of the fog and ordered a return to the scene at full speed. They pulled as many people as they could find aboard the damaged *Ogdensburg,* but almost three hundred people, many of them the hapless immigrants, either went down with the ship or drowned while waiting rescue. The *Atlantic* went to the bottom some four miles off Long Point in 155 feet of water.

Meanwhile, the remarkable underwater achievements of Johnny Green had made dramatic fare in the newspapers along the lake, and before the summer was out he was approached by a Mr. Wells and a Mr. Malefoot, representing the American Express Company. Their company, the pair explained, was the owner of the $36,000 in the *Atlantic's* safe; they indicated that a handsome reward would be forthcoming if Green would recover it. Another $700, they pointed out, was in a trunk in the adjacent captain's office.

Readily agreeing to the project although the reported position of the wreck was at an unheard of depth for the diving gear of the day, Green joined the two other divers the firm had already hired and went to the scene of the wreck. The sunken hulk was found, but when the depth was plumbed and found to be actually 165 feet, the two saltwater divers flatly refused to work.

In this strained atmosphere of disappointment and distrust, Johnny Green climbed into his suit and weights. The location of the safe had not yet been revealed. Green gave a significant lifting of the eyebrows to the nervous Mr. Wells.

Wells, giving a furtive glance around, leaned over and whispered, "Port side, one deck down and the third window aft the wheelhouse!"

Nodding, the diver ordered his copper helmet screwed on and went over the side. The first descent was nearly the last. Green found himself inside the *Atlantic's* big funnel! At this point the air hose burst and he signaled for an emergency ascent. Three more times that day he was lowered to the hulk only to find that the air pumps were not capable of supplying enough air at that depth. On the fourth descent, after repairs and changes, he landed on the ship's walking beam and in the total darkness that existed at that depth began to feel his way to the deck. But once again an air line burst, and this time it was necessary to return to Buffalo for more hose and pump repairs. On their return to the wreck he went down several times, but the pumps still would not supply enough air to keep the suit inflated below the waist. Almost crushed by the pressure, and suffering severe pains in his legs, Green was forced to limit his dives to thirty minutes.

Wells, discouraged at the lack of progress and bad weather that kept them away from the wreck for days at a time, finally ordered the salvage attempt abandoned.

But the *Atlantic's* safe had become a challenge to Johnny Green, and from then on it was to become a consuming passion. He made a mental resolution to return again to the wreck, this time with his own expedition, after the legal statutes of elapsed time, three years in this instance, had brought the wreck and everything it contained within the public domain.

During the winter of 1854–1855, which he spent in Boston, Green designed and built two improved diving suits, suits that proved so successful in saltwater tests that the Boston Wrecking Company hired him to do the diving on an expedition to the West Indies, there to explore the wreck of the British man-of-war, *Soverign,* lost on the Silver Banks in 1773. The *Soverign* proving unrewarding, the group moved on, investigating and exploring a dozen other wrecks, none of which yielded more than military equipment or historical curios.

It was August of 1855 when Johnny Green, aboard the salvage schooner *Yorktown,* returned to the grave of the *Atlantic;* August 20, to be exact, three years and one day after the ship went down—the first day, legally, that the ship and her treasure belonged to him who was bold enough to take it!

Strangely, he reported to his tenders after his first trial descent, the ship had changed position, her bow having shifted from southwest to southeast. And in the three years he had been gone some ten inches of mud had accumulated on her decks and superstructure.

After groping around for several days, during which time he suffered some pain, sensations of dizziness and drowsiness, he felt his way from the wheelhouse down to the next deck and then along the rail. Thus, on the morning of August 23, he reached through the third window aft the wheelhouse and felt the comforting and cold bulk of the long-sought safe! Surfacing immediately, he called for an iron bar and a saw. It was a sweltering day on the surface, and while he waited Green quaffed deeply and downed a hearty meal. Down below again he cut and pried away enough of the cabin bulkhead to permit him to drag and push the safe out. He left it between the cabin and the railing while he went up again to fashion lifting hooks to attach to the heavy iron handles on each side of the safe. The prize he had sought for so long was now his . . . almost.

Back on the deck of the *Yorktown* he had barely removed his helmet when he was wracked with excruciating pain. In moments he was semiconscious and almost completely paralyzed! Johnny Green had a bad case of the "bends!" Rushed immediately to Port Dover, where two doctors said he could not possibly live, he had improved slightly by nightfall, and the decision was made to take him to Buffalo, where it was felt the doctors might have had more experience with the dread affliction.

In the Buffalo hospital a puzzled nurse reported to her supervisor that the patient's almost incoherent ramblings seemed to be about "a third window, somewhere aft of something called a wheelhouse."

Sent home to Boston in late September, he lay in his bed for five months before any improvement was evident. After six months he was able to move slightly and by summer could walk a few steps with the help of crutches.

Sick, crippled and unable to dive himself, Green returned again to the wreck of the *Atlantic* in July of 1856, fitting out a vessel and hiring two supposedly experienced and fearless divers. But something was amiss at the wreck site. The line he had carefully secured to the railing beside the safe and the buoy he had adjusted to float just under the surface were both gone! Quickly he ordered the divers to dress for the descent. If luck was with him for a change, the safe would be aboard the schooner in a half hour! The divers, however, experienced a sudden change of heart about going down to that depth or anything close to it. But Johnny Green was not about to be beaten this time with the prize so near. Still partially crippled and paralyzed, he climbed into a suit and ordered the tenders to lower him. This time he struck the wreck on the hurricane deck and again felt his way forward to the wheelhouse, down one deck and back to the third window aft, in such pain that he had to crawl most of the way.

But the *Atlantic*'s safe was gone! Sick at heart as well as physically, he fought his way slowly to the stateroom where the trunk with $700 was supposed to be. It was gone, too!

Broken now in spirit as well as in body, Green was drawn to the surface, where he suffered another attack of the bends. This time he was taken directly to Buffalo for treatment, but from then until the day he died Johnny Green carried the marks of the diver who has gone too deep and has stayed too long, a bent and twisted body and permanent partial paralysis of the limbs.

While recovering in Buffalo he suffered the cruelest blow of all. A rival diver, Elliott P. Harrington, he learned, had brought up the *Atlantic*'s safe on June 27, the very day the Green expedition had sailed for the wreck site!

Harrington, of Volusia, New York, with Charles Gardner and Martin Quigley of nearby Chautauqua and William Newton of Detroit, Michigan, had formed their own salvage team to get the *Atlantic*'s safe without any prior agreement with the American Express Company. Working from the schooner *Fletcher,* they arrived at a point about three miles off the west end of Long Point on the afternoon of June 18. Apparently they had dragged and located the wreck previously, for they knew exactly where to go. Moored over the hulk, they spent the rest of the day preparing for the adventure, testing pumps, lines and gear.

On the morning of June 19, Harrington donned his Wells-McGowan diving suit, buckled 248 pounds of lead around him and went over the side. On the first descent he landed squarely on the *Atlantic*'s promenade deck at a spot he figured about 40 feet abaft the long sought third stateroom aft the wheelhouse on the port side. He stayed on the deck only one minute. The pressure was great and the water so cold he was unable to distinguish glass from metal or wood. He estimated that about four inches of silt had accumulated on the decks and reported to his helpers that once below 50 feet he had been in total darkness, working entirely by touch. The pressure, he said, "Made sparks seem to shoot from my eyes." In all he made four short dives that first day, staying down a little longer each time. And after the first one he carried with him a small steel bar. If he hit something and it broke he concluded it was glass. If it was unyielding it was part of the bulkheading or a door.

On June 20 Harrington made four more trips down to the treasure ship and on the last one located the third stateroom aft the wheelhouse. He had spent a total of thirty-five minutes on the deck of the *Atlantic!*

According to his account he spent thirty-seven minutes working under water on the third day of salvaging, during which time he entered the stateroom through a window, got a line through a ring on the safe and dragged it to the side of the cabin. With the steel bar he had broken away some of the woodwork but found the aperture still too small to pass the safe through. He then suspended work for that day. The safe was obviously in an anteroom of the purser's office, having no door opening directly to the deck, for neither Green nor Harrington mentioned a door which would have simplified the problem.

With the surface of Lake Erie a flat calm on Sunday, June 22, Harrington went down to the *Atlantic* for the sixteenth time. It took him only seven minutes to saw away the window casing and some of the paneling around it. On the second dive he placed a line on the loosened woodwork and had it drawn to the surface and out of his way. The third dive of that fateful Sunday was the last. This time he tied a line to the safe and, clinging to it, was drawn to the surface. Thus Elliott Harrington bade farewell to the *Atlantic!*

On the *Fletcher*'s foredeck the excited salvagers pried open the safe, actually a sizeable stongbox, since it measued only 28 by 18 by 16 inches. In it they found $5000 in gold coin, $31,000 in bills and six gold watches. At least, that was the inventory given by Harrington in Cleveland, Ohio, on July 7. It failed to list some of the other known items reported to be in it, namely a parcel of Michigan State Bonds and a warrant on the United States Treasury drawn in favor of John N. Gains, Paymaster, United States Army, for $10,000. It bore the number 2841 and was dated August 11, 1852, less than ten days before the *Atlantic* took her plunge.

The coin and currency were divided among the salvagers,

but the American Express Company quickly claimed this to be contrary to law and, through their Buffalo attorney, asked a United States Court to confiscate the hard-earned loot. In the end the company offered a compromise and, since they apparently had a point of law on their side that the salvagers had been unfamiliar with, it was accepted. They could have fought the issue, perhaps successfully, but they had no desire to forfeit any of their gains in attorney's fees. Each of the four was awarded an even share of the gold coin and $2000 in currency, a grand total of about $7000.

Harrington, however, lost a good share of his currency when he tried to dry it in his mother's kitchen stove. A diver he was; a drier of bills he was not.

Agonizingly disappointed, Johnny Green called attention to some of Harrington's claims and pointed out some obvious discrepancies, particularly in the dates given. He recalled too that in his dives on the *Atlantic* he had never encountered total darkness, even at the depth of nearly 165 feet where the wreck lay. Nor, claimed Green, did Harrington find the safe or strongbox in a stateroom, since he (Green) had only the year before removed part of the cabin paneling before pulling it outside the room and to the rail of the ship, fastening a line to it so that it could be easily located on the next dive. And what about the trunk with the $700? It was gone when Green made his last dive, but Harrington made no mention of it. Did the *Atlantic* have another visitor?

A lesser man would have been content to spend the rest of his days ashore nurturing the bitter seeds of self-pity and defeat, but Johnny Green was of another breed. In the spring of 1857 he outfitted another small salvage vessel and headed for Lake Huron where, in the area of Thunder Bay Island, Middle Island Reef and Presque Isle, the bottom was littered with freight, machinery and heavy deck cargoes jettisoned by vessels in distress. However, being unable to dive himself or hire efficient underwater men, he found the business unprofitable. Early in the summer he headed for Lake Erie again, where the wreck of a steamer lying some miles off Cleveland was rumored to hold some gold and a valuable cargo of tools and machinery.

Lake Erie was in a violent mood the day the salvage craft arrived at the wreck scene. The anchors began to drag after Green attempted to swing his vessel into the wind. Seas began to sweep over the deck and some of the precious pumps and diving gear went adrift, sliding from side to side and causing heavy damage.

Green frantically ordered the anchors hoisted and began a perilous dash for Cleveland. He had almost won the fight when a huge sea dashed the ship against one of the entrance piers, where it quickly filled and sank! Thus ended the active career of Johnny Green, salvager!

Even in retirement and poor health Green was the accepted expert in underwater exploration. Everywhere he went people wanted to hear of his adventures, particularly the sad saga of the *Atlantic*. At the suggestion of friends he set to work on a small book detailing his life and work under the surface of the lakes and oceans. Published in Buffalo by Faxon's Steam Power Press, the book, *Diving With and Without Armor*, or *The Submarine Exploits of J. B. Green, the Celebrated Submarine Diver*, sold well. But it was an era when underwater exploration was still a fascinating novelty holding an almost compulsive aura of romance. Many a callow city youth and sturdy farm boy devoured the book page by page, envisioning the day when he, like J. B. Green, the Celebrated Submarine Diver, could probe the mysteries of the seas. When the Civil War came along the drama of the battlefield soon relegated the book to the musty back shelves, and Johnny Green was forgotten by all but the great fraternity of men who sailed the lakes. For years he wandered from port to port, sometimes performing menial tasks to justify his passage but often just going along for the ride, no questions asked or passage money expected.

Charles H. Wescott, who later became supervising inspector of steam vessels for the Eighth Coast Guard District, recalled that in 1865, as cabin boy on the old steamer *Forest Queen,* he often heard Green tell of his dives to the *Atlantic.*

"He made many trips with us that year," Wescott said, "Captain Ward had given orders that he should be taken without charge wherever he wanted to go."

History fails to record the last resting place of Johnny Green, but the accepted story, handed down from one generation of seamen to another is that poor old Johnny, tired and twisted of body, died in a humble sailor's bunk aboard an aged package freighter beating her way down Lake Erie one night. He had been telling the fo'c'sle crew his famous stories of the sunken treasure, the story goes. They say his faded blue eyes were alight and his voice steady when he recounted the experiences and emotions of his last dive to the wreck. At the moment the old freighter was proceeding through heavy fog off Long Point, her whistle bleating ominously. Johnny Green sighed deeply and lay back on his pillow—dead!

Who can deny that the spirits of the dead had reached up to take him once more to the shifting hulk of the *Atlantic* ". . . one deck down and three windows aft the wheelhouse."

# 4

⚓

## *The Sunken Sisters*

Whenever new methods, new materials and new ideas invade an industry of vast scope there is an era of transition in which a certain trial-and-error period is inevitable. In the business of shipbuilding it is a time when, as a patriarch of the industry once phrased it

We learn by doing and the results of that doing, the things we cannot possibly glean from the slide rule, the drafting board or, for that matter, the engineering laboratories, the mold loft or the fabricating shops. Not even when these combined skills result in a newer or bigger ship do we know for certain what we have wrought. Only when the end product performs well the several difficult tasks her owners demand of her can we say that we have advanced.

The period of transition from wooden ships to iron was fraught with suspicion and distrust. Like their saltwater counterparts, lake sailors were slow to accept the inevitable shift to iron hulls. It is well to be able to sit at a desk with a mass of statistics and graphs, they argued, but still another thing to be on a ship laboring in heavy seas, watching her

54

hull flex and twist and her masts arc in opposite directions as the wave action suspends the hull between continually varying crests. They knew wood could take the bending and pulling, but iron, as a hull material, had still to be proved.

By the 1880's the era of general package freight was on the wane, and the iron ore trade had been firmly established as the largest tonnage factor in Great Lakes shipping. Now ships were being designed to carry large bulk cargoes of ore. The design, happily, was equally efficient for other bulk cargoes such as limestone and coal. Ease of loading and unloading inspired the typical lake freighter profile of today with engines aft and navigating houses forward. With intense competition prevailing, owners were demanding larger, faster and more economical vessels. Only the hardy and venturesome survived as the lake shipping industry gradually shifted, as the medical men would put it, from general practice to specialization.

So it came about in 1882, despite doubts and predictions, that the first specifically designed ore carrier to be built of iron, the *Onoko,* slipped down the ways in the yards of the Globe Iron Works in Cleveland. She was slightly over 302 feet long, 39 feet wide, 25 feet in depth and her cavernous holds accommodated three thousand tons of ore. Contrary to all the dire prognostications of the skeptics, the *Onoko* was an almost instant success. Before she had completed her first six trips orders were being placed at many yards for similar ships of iron.

Among those ordering new steamers were Captain Peter G. Minch and J. C. Gilchrist. Captain Minch had succeeded to the helm of his father's business. The elder Minch had been financially interested in the *Onoko* and managed or owned several other ships. The new Minch ship, the *Western Reserve,* official number 81294, slid down the ways of the Cleveland Shipbuilding Company in 1890, having a gross tonnage of 2392, a keel of 300 feet, 7 inches, and a beam of 41 feet, 2 inches. A year later, in the same yards, the Gilchrist vessel, the *W. H. Gilcher,* official number 81326, was duly launched and christened. While there were very slight differences in dimensions and fittings, the two vessels were so alike that they were commonly called "sister" ships despite their separate fleet affiliations. Both were given A-1 classifications.

Each vessel immediately lived up to its owner's fondest expectations in respect to speed and efficiency. Indeed, the *Gilcher* almost at once captured a grain-carrying record by transporting 113,885 bushels of wheat from Chicago to Buffalo, largest wheat cargo carried to that date. The *Western Reserve,* meanwhile, was concentrating on iron ore.

In late August of 1882, Captain Minch, whose duties ashore made him restless, invited his family and some close relatives to accompany him on the *Western Reserve,* bound light from Cleveland to Two Harbors, Minnesota, for iron ore. Those aboard as the ship passed through the Soo and into Whitefish Bay, in addition to the crew, were Captain Minch, his wife, Anna, his son Charlie and daughter Florence, and Mrs. Minch's sister Mrs. Jacob Delker Englebry and her daughter Bertha. Like the Englebrys, the Minch family was from Vermilion, Ohio, as were Captain Albert Myers, his son Carl and several crew members.

A summer storm was churning the waters of Whitefish Bay on the afternoon of August 30, and Captain Myers, bearing in mind that the ship was without either cargo or water ballast but also certain in his own mind that his vessel was practically new and as sturdy as the science of shipbuilding could make it, drove her on. But at about nine o'clock that night, when she was approximately sixty miles above the point, the *Western Reserve* simply broke in two!

Captain Minch, his family and guests and some of the

crew took to the wooden lifeboat, the rest of the crew launching a metallic yawl. The ship went down in minutes, but even before she disappeared the metal lifesaving yawl capsized. Only two of its occupants, Captain Myer's son and the steward, managed to climb into the wooden boat!

The frightening story of the *Western Reserve*'s structural failure and the terrible night in the wooden lifeboat might have been just another in the long list of Lake Superior mysteries but for the story told by young Harry W. Stewart, wheelsman, who fought his way through the breakers off Deer Park the next morning.

Some days after the disaster, as part of an important ritual that has many implications and ramifications in the insurance and shipbuilding industries, Harry W. Stewart appeared in Cleveland to give and sign his official statement and several legal documents pertaining to the sinking. Officials responsible for affixing the cause and determining factors that may have led to the loss of a vessel only two years old were favorably impressed by the young wheelsman. The *Marine Review*, the "Bible" of the lakes shipping industry, described him as "An elegant specimen of physical manhood, and of bright, shrewd manner." And as a matter of record the publication printed a copy of his sworn statement:

We had locked through the Sault after dinner, August 30, passed Whitefish Point about four o'clock and adopted the usual course to clear Keweenaw Point. Wind was westerly with a sea running more from northwest, increasing. The affiant [signer of a deposition] went into his room forward about seven o'clock. Up till nine o'clock the sea was very heavy, causing the vessel to labor and occasionally pound very hard, but making good weather. At the hour mentioned there was a violent, jolting shock and jar, followed by the noise of a spar breaking and falling on deck. Affiant started up and Capt. Myers came and called out to get out quickly, she would sink. Affiant partially dressed, hurried out and ran aft on the port side of the vessel.

There was a break in the deck forward of the mainmast and the mainmast was broken off somewhere near the middle, the broken part lying on deck. The night was very dark. The wind had died down for a shift of wind but the sea was very heavy. Both boats were launched, one on the port and the other on the starboard. Into the starboard boat there got Captain Minch, managing owner, his wife and two children, his sister-in-law and her child . . . all of them making the trip with us . . . and Capt. Myers and others of the crew, in all seventeen in that boat. We picked up the other wheelsman who had failed to get into either boat, and in a short time we picked up another man who reported that the other boat had capsized. We saw and heard the steamer go down with a great noise. The wind as before stated had died down with a shift of wind and in a very short time it came up again, from the N.N.W., blowing hard, and throughout the night the sea seemed to increase. The steamer went down nearly sixty miles from Whitefish Point, according to Capt. Myers' calculations. The sea was so heavy that it was simply impossible to do anything but to head our boat right before wind and seas. We tried to keep her up but could not do it. The water was coming over her side so we had to bale constantly, even while running before it. We thus ran for ten hours making about thirty miles when, at seven o'clock in the morning of the 31st, when perhaps a mile off the beach, a succession of heavy seas caught our boat, lifting her nearly on end, filled her as she came down, and capsized her, throwing all into the water. With the aid of a life preserver which I found and fastened on in the water, I made my way through the breakers and reached land about ten miles above Deer Park. The others all perished.

Meanwhile, the victims of the *Western Reserve* tragedy were coming ashore in the pounding cold surf west of the lifesaving station. They were buried as they were found by Captain Frahm's crew from the station, in carefully marked graves in the sand high above the beach. Landmarks were carefully noted so that relatives who wished to claim the bodies might do so.

In telegrams to Philip Minch from Captain Frahm the names and brief descriptions were as follows:

First body buried . . . Man supposed to be between thirty and forty-five years old. Six feet, sandy mustache, bald on top of head, probably an engineer or steward. Buried eight miles west of station.

Second . . . Man supposed to be thirty years old, dark hair, small sandy mustache, about 5 feet, 10 inches, weight about 175, probably fireman or oiler. Buried 8¼ miles west of station.

Third . . . Man from twenty-five to thirty, blonde; probably a deck hand. Buried 10 miles west of station.

Fourth . . . Deck hand or fireman, about 155 pounds, supposed to be thirty-five years of age, dark complexion. Buried 12½ miles west of station.

Fifth . . . Body supposed to be Schuyler Steward of Algonac, Mich. Buried 6½ miles west of station.

Sixth . . . Body found 11 miles west of station. No description furnished yet.

At the time of the telegrams, seventeen bodies had been recovered, five of the seventeen being those of passengers. Ten were still to be accounted for, including second mate Charles LeBeau, chief engineer W. H. Seamen, second engineer Charles Wills, steward Bert Smith, assistant steward George Davis and oiler Robert Simpson.

The *Marine Review* commented in print:

After filling the graves, the captain ordered his crew to kneel as he offered up a prayer. There may have been more eloquent sermons preached in some churches . . . but probably none more sincere than the simple prayers uttered on the desert shore of Lake Superior over the form of an unknown fireman or deck hand.

As usual when a ship founders, particularly when it is known, as from wheelsman Stewart's account, that structural failure had been at fault, there are numerous pertinent questions asked by those in authority to determine where the responsibility lies. It is only by patient probing that mistakes are rectified, designs corrected and new aspects of stress and strain revealed.

Quite logically then, the *Western Reserve*'s builders came in for some harsh and often bitter criticism. But like others, they were at a loss to explain the complete fracturing of the hull and, almost immediately, submitted the vessel's plans to other shipbuilders for study and comment. Without exception, all agreed that there was no evidence of possible structural weakness apparent in the design. For that matter, had not wheelsman Stewart lived to tell of the ship's last moments, the *Western Reserve* would simply have been listed as another missing vessel, her disappearance as mysterious as others that preceded her!

The seeds of doubt now planted by the survivor's grim testimony as to the condition of the sea and vessel, operators of new steel ships at once issued orders to their masters not to drive their high-powered vessels into a head sea when the vessel was without cargo or adequate ballast.

Two months later, while the furor in shipbuilding circles was still raging, the *W. H. Gilcher* was steaming westbound through the Straits of Mackinac in the dusk of a wild day, bound for Milwaukee with three thousand long tons of coal in her holds. Steering well clear of Grays Reef, Captain Leeds H. Weeks set a course that would carry him down the lake east of North and South Manitou Islands before turning almost directly westward on the Milwaukee course. A former shipwright himself, Captain Weeks was a master of long experience, having commanded five schooners and three steamers in the Gilchrist line before bringing out the

*Gilcher.* If there had ever been any doubt in his mind as to the *Gilcher*'s structural qualities he had never expressed them. Evidence that he was completely satisfied with his ship is borne out by the fact that he, like the owner of the *Western Reserve,* was from Vermilion and had "signed on" a crew consisting of a number of his fellow townspeople. These facts notwithstanding, it is a simple matter of record that the *W. H. Gilcher,* on the night of October 28, 1892, vanished from the face of Lake Michigan!

In cases such as those of missing ships, the more searching, embarrassing questions are more likely to be asked not in a musty coroner's office, but in the waterfront taprooms, the ship chandlers' lofts, the shipbuilding yards and in the offices of government agencies whose duties deal with the standards for shipbuilding, the equipping of vessels with proper safety devices and the qualifications of the men who sail on them. Since many men then sailing had still to be convinced of the merits of steel over wooden hulls and were extremely vocal in their doubts, the loss of the *Gilcher* and *Western Reserve* could not simply be brushed off by calling them victims of the "inevitable hazards of the sea."

"Could it be," they asked, "that a monumental error in the making of the steel for the two ships resulted in a product that was too brittle to take the flexing and twisting given a ship working in a seaway?"

Since neither vessel was available to become "Exhibit A" in the ensuing hearings, the question was never answered and probably never will be.

Official probers, however, were quick to point out that it was highly unlikely that the *Gilcher* had suffered structural failure since, unlike the *Western Reserve,* she had a full cargo of three thousand tons of coal, which would serve to stiffen and strengthen her against undue stress and strain. Ironically, the old wooden steamer *John F. Eddy* and the

line steamer *Albany* had both been in the same area on the
night of October 28 and had come through the storm un-
scathed, although the masters of both ships reported tremendous seas and poor visibility throughout the night.

"It may be more than a coincidence, too," the investigators
said, "that the schooner *Ostrich,* also with a coal cargo in
her holds, disappeared on Lake Michigan the same night.
Since the weather was unusually heavy around midnight,
the possibility of a collision is not to be dismissed lightly!"

The thirty-six-year-old *Ostrich,* Captain McKay owner and
master, was registered at 279 gross tons with a length of 139
feet. She was headed for Milwaukee, her home port, with a
crew of six.

But a collision leaves wreckage, usually plenty of it, and
a big new steel ship is not quickly cut down by a plodding
old schooner. There would have been time to don life
jackets, lower boats, cast overboard life buoys or get clear of
the ship in some manner!

Later that fall, Captain Stuffelbaum of the steam barge
*Hattie B. Perene* found small pieces of wreckage on High
Island, bits of which were identified as the "stringbacks"
that supported the canvas covers on the *Gilcher's* lifeboats.
They had been slashed with an ax, indicating that whatever
fate befell the *Gilcher* it came with such calamitous rapidity
that the men rushing to the boats did not even take time
to rip back the canvas covers in the usual manner. Since
the boats were never found it was assumed they were never
launched. Near the "stringbacks" were bits of wreckage
from a sailing craft, a mishmash of jetsam that could or
could not have come from the *Ostrich*. Wreckage from
schooners was common enough on the shores of Lake Michigan's islands. It could have come from the *Ostrich* or any
one of the dozen lost that year or the year before.

On the subject of lifeboats, the editor of the *Marine Record* had a few pertinent words. Said he on May 8, 1901:

It seems to us that perhaps these little lifeboats are not all that could be desired for life-saving purposes. Now that vessels are compelled to carry metal lifeboats it should be determined whether they save or take life, to be so named. In this connection we have also in view the fate of the crews of the lake steamers *Western Reserve* and *Gilcher,* both having metal lifeboats, but no lives saved.

Strangely, no bodies of either the *Gilcher* or *Ostrich* crews were ever found, but up on Whitefish Point those of the *Western Reserve* floated slowly in, like penitent children fearful of being scolded for being absent without leave. They were found along the beach from two to twenty-two miles from Deer Park Lifesaving Station. But even as the station's surfmen dug graves above the sandy beach and knelt in prayer at each, the furor ashore continued.

Owners contemplating new ships wanted assurances that their vessels would not suffer similar fates; builders feared that the unexplained disasters would seriously curtail the building of the types of ships they were now physically equipped to build; insurance underwriters shuddered at the potential tremendous losses to be incurred; the seamen, still convinced that steel would not stand the test of stress and strain at sea, complained bitterly that the lives of their ship-mates were being sacrificed in the mad race to build steel ships while they, the men who must man them, paid the price of experimentation.

The argument that Captain Peter G. Minch would hardly have risked his own life as well as those of his family and relatives had he suspected weakness in his vessel carried little weight.

"Why," demanded the adamant seamen, "did the *Onoko,*

actually slightly longer but not as wide as the *Western Reserve* and *Gilcher,* prove so successful while the latter vessels broke up or disappeared in less than two years? Was it the steel, the design, or the combination of both?"

Perhaps the answer is to be found in the fact that in the nine years between the *Onoko's* building in 1882, and the *Western Reserve* in 1890 and the *Gilcher* in 1891, vast changes were taking place in America's steel industry. The *Onoko* was built of iron, which has tremendous resiliency to bending, twisting and deterioration. Indeed, ironwork from wrecks that have lain underwater for two centuries has been tested and found to have lost little or none of the original qualities. Making iron was a slow and expensive process. Steel was almost prohibitive in cost. What the steel mills were crying for was a less expensive way of making steel, and they found it in the Bessemer process. Steel production and tonnage output skyrocketed. Steel, once so precious and expensive that its use was restricted to sharp cutting instruments and tools, was now available in almost unlimited quantities. Overjoyed shipbuilders were quick to switch to its use. Perhaps too quick. One gathers that the steel men, concentrating on what they considered the ultimate and universal product for thousands of uses, overlooked the fact that ship steel must have special metallurgical and physical properties that might not necessarily apply to railroad rails, bridges or skyscraper frames.

Lloyds of London, the great marine insurers, have carefully prescribed what must go into a vessel if they are to classify and insure her. Their naval architects examine the plans carefully, and their surveyors inspect the ship frequently while she is building. Not only do they set rigid and inflexible rules of construction but they specify certain exacting standards for the material that goes into her, particularly the steel in her hull and framing. These rules have been universally adopted and standardized the world over and are the working specifications of many agencies involved in ship construction and classification, regardless of the insurer.

All the rules do not apply in the case of the *Western Reserve* and *Gilcher,* although both were classed A-1, but four of them are of special significance when applied to the circumstances surrounding the fate of the two vessels. These are the rules whose application was supposedly incumbent upon the Cleveland Rolling Mill Company, fabricators of the steel for both hulls, and the surveyor whose duties required him to witness the tests.

Rule No. 10, for example, states that, "Strips cut lengthwise or crosswise of the plate to have ultimate tensile strength of not less than 28 and more than 32 long tons per square inch of section with an elongation equal to at least 16 per cent on a length of eight inches before fracture."

Rule No. 11 "Steel angles intended for framing of vessels and bulb steel for beams may have maximum tensile strength of 33 tons per square inch of section provided they be capable of standing the bending tests, and of being efficiently welded."

Rule No. 12 "Strips cut from plate angle or bulb steel to be heated to low cherry red and cooled in water of 82 degrees, Fahrenheit, must stand bending double around a curve of which the diameter is not more than three times the thickness of the plates tested."

Rule No. 13 "In addition to this, samples of plates and bars should be subjected to cold bending tests at the discretion of the surveyors."

The question posed by many was very simple. Did the steel in the *Western Reserve* and *Gilcher* measure up to these exacting tests or was it subjected to a more cursory examination, if indeed, it was tested at all?

Many interested and qualified individuals never wavered from their opinions that the steel was faulty. One of them, Fred A. Ballin, a naval architect with the Detroit Boat Works, made grave charges in a paper he later read to a convention of naval architects. Said Ballin, in reference to his own firm's experience with the new Bessemer steel:

We found it almost impossible to get a homogenous stock of steel even in the same plate. We had lab tests made and found that the plates and angles would crack in handling, heating or punching. . . . We seriously considered the probability of returning to iron. . . .

We then, 7 years ago, came to the conclusion that the steel [Bessemer] made to Lloyd's test was unfit for ship building.

Savings in the Bessemer process might save money . . . about $12,000 in a ship with a 310-foot hull line . . . a tidy fortune to be saved when a builder uses the newer process with the surveyor's acquiescence!

Whatever naval architect Ballin's reasoning processes were, he must have had cold facts on his side, for even today Bessemer-process steel is not recognized as ship quality by any of the various classification societies. They require open-hearth or electric-furnace stock, and even then individual metallurgical properties are specified for various thicknesses of plates or framing stock!

It is significant, too, in the light of Ballin's harsh words, to point out that the old *Onoko,* prototype of the armada of larger vessels that were to follow her and built of iron instead of Bessemer steel, was in active service for thirty-three years before foundering in Lake Superior.

Assuming then that there may have been faulty steel in both the *Western Reserve* and *Gilcher,* it is in the realm of possibility that the *Gilcher* could have developed small cracks and fractures in her plates and framing—defects that went unnoticed until too late. She would be ripe then for disaster when caught in a gale of the severity of the one that lashed Lake Michigan that October night. But Captain Weeks was too experienced a shipmaster to have ignored the fact that his vessel might quite likely have the same weaknesses as her sister ship. They were alike as two peas in a pod, and Weeks, with his own shipbuilding experience behind him, would undoubtedly have surveyed his own craft inside and out between cargoes. He must have had every confidence in the *Gilcher,* for after transiting the Straits of Mackinac he could, as other shipmasters did that night, have anchored in the lee of Beaver Island. Instead he chose to continue down Lake Michigan.

There is shoal water immediately south of South Fox Island, and a heavily laden vessel, driven off her course in a gale, could easily encounter grief there, as many have. If this had been the case the *Gilcher* would have quickly been broken up by the 30-foot seas that marched on the lake that night. This being the case, there would have been wreckage other than the lifeboat "stringbacks." Nothing was found such as could have been expected had her cabins and deckhouse been torn off, her below-decks areas gutted as the hull disintegrated or the crew swept away. There would have been wooden paneling, furniture, mattresses, life buoys or even the buoyant metallic lifeboats. Always, when a ship disappears literally without a trace, there are rumors of uncharted reefs or rocks—underwater hazards that in fair weather offer no problem but that, to a vessel down to her marks and dropping in the trough of 30-foot seas, would serve as a giant can opener. The end would come swiftly, especially to a ship with brittle steel in her!

For weeks after the *Gilcher* disappeared the area in which she apparently foundered was systematically swept. But the search vessels found no rocks or shoals other than those already known and charted. Nor, for that matter, did they find the *Gilcher.*

Thanks to the *Western Reserve*'s hardy wheelsman, Harry W. Stewart, there was no mystery involved in his ship's passing. But what of the *Gilcher?*

In all likelihood the mystery of the *Gilcher* will never be solved, for she lies in deep water, one of a great phantom fleet where only the ghosts of lost sailors tramp the decks of vanished ships!

Tangled in the cluster of wreckage that drifted ashore from the broken *Western Reserve* was the vessel's green starboard running light. For as long as he lived the late Captain Philip Minch, another son of Captain Peter G. Minch, kept it burning continuously in the den of his Mentor, Ohio, home in honor of the *Western Reserve*'s dead. When he passed on, the light went to "Lawnfield," the President Garfield home and museum, also in Mentor. It hangs from a roof gable there today, still burning. But it is only a curiosity to those who know nothing of its sad story.

# 5

⚓

# *What's in a Name?*

Sailors the world over and for time immemorial are a clannish, superstitious, hard-to-understand lot. Their adversities ashore, whatever the nature, are accepted philosophically; their calamities afloat, probably because, for the time being, she is their life, their home and their means of sustenance, are the fault of the ship. The blame for the bad or credit for the good is, by tradition and legend, attributed to the ship's spiritual disposition, supposedly inherent in the timbers or plates of a vessel the day her keel is laid.

If a ship has better than average passages, is blessed with cargoes that do not shift, answers swiftly and surely to her helm, "feeds" her crew well and keeps dry 'tween decks in nasty weather, she earns her reputation as a "good" ship by those best qualified to pass judgment—her fo'c'sle crew. If, however, her voyages are a succession of wet decks, cantankerous cargoes, fouled lines and damage claims and if she tends to yaw easily or is slow recovering from rolls, the same inflexible court up for'ard renders a judgment of "jinx." The verdict, again by legend and tradition, follows her for-

ever through a lifetime of unhappy voyages until at last she
founders or is towed sullenly to the breaker's yard.

In the case of the jinx decree, those among the fo'c'sle, and
sailors have notoriously long memories, can always trace her
history and performance back to some ill-omened happening
that, among the superstitious, supposedly doomed her from
the very beginning—a black cat seen in the shipyard on
launching day, her keel having been laid on a Friday or a
crosseyed man aboard during her builder's trials.

So there it is, term it what one will—superstition, plain
bad luck or ignorance. But the fact remains that some ships
have a predilection for trouble, a sequence of adversities that
never ends. Sailor's yarns or superstitions carry little weight,
however, in the higher echelons of the shipping industry.
Those who own, manage or charter vessels know that when
a ship fails to perform as her owners and builders intended,
the fault more likely rests in a poor design. Too much or too
little beam for her length, niggardliness in her power plant
or poorly placed machinery can cause a ship to yaw or be
overly tender in a seaway. Rarely does a jinx ship mend her
ways unless, in subsequent years, she is the subject of major
structural changes. She is either "good" or "jinx," and in
either event the temper of her crew and the pocketbook of
her owners will make the final judgment in a court that
never reverses a decision.

On saltwater, through centuries of commerce, when the
jinx sentence has been passed, it has been the ship itself that
carries the burden, an unenviable cross to be borne with as
much dignity as she can muster for the rest of her days.
Crews are hard to find and harder to keep, for the fo'c'sle
scuttlebutt of the seas can be a malignant and seemingly endless curse.

Conversely, and for no explainable or plausible reason,
the jinx verdict on the Great Lakes seems to follow a pattern

of ship names rather than the ships—a likely enough name often being foredoomed to a succession of misfortunes although over the years, it may be bestowed on a number of vessels of various kinds and with different owners. Fires, strandings, collisions and founderings have been their sorry lot with uncanny consistency.

A case in point is the name *Oneida,* which in various instances has honored a tribe of Indians, a city and a lake in New York state. But however honorable and distinguished, the name *Oneida* brought tragedy and misfortune to several vessels, beginning with a 227-ton sidewheel steamer that abruptly sank in Lake Erie after only a couple of seasons in service. Three years later a schooner of the same name was wrecked and lost in a thundering gale off Chicago, spreading her wreckage along fifteen miles of beach. Next came a steamer of 345 tons, and she, like her predecessors, capsized in a howling Lake Erie gale, with a loss of nineteen lives. One would think that owners would pause before again burdening any vessel with so unlucky a name. But past history didn't deter a Buffalo group from building a 887-ton steamer and naming her, in quite ostentatious ceremonies, the *Oneida.* She, too, after several unprofitable seasons during which she jousted with docks, sandbars, shoals and other vessels, caught fire and burned to the water line, again in Lake Erie!

The name *Racine* does honor to a French dramatic poet and a fair city in Wisconsin. It is a short, pleasant, happy-sounding name, but none of these intangible attributes was inherited by vessels that carried the name. The first was a brig that promptly foundered off the Wisconsin shore. The second *Racine* was a steamer, built in Oswego, New York. After a season or two, during which she exhibited a deplorable tendency to be overtender, she was converted into a sailing craft. This failed to cure her outrageous rolling and slow recoveries in any kind of sea, and she was soon lost in a relatively mild gale. Then came another propeller ship named *Racine,* and she, as if following a preordained course of disaster, caught fire off Rondeau, Ontario, eight of her crew perishing in the flames. The name was then given to a big schooner, but the switch back to sail from steam failed to discourage whatever evil spirit haunted the name. She was wrecked and lost on Lake Huron in 1892!

*"Queen of the Lakes"* is a name any proud owner might be tempted to bestow on a new vessel. In fact, several did. The name indicates supremacy in size and performance, but grim tales of tragedy have relentlessly followed it on the Great Lakes. The first was a 563-ton steamer, seemingly destined for a long and useful life. But one night, while docked at Marquette, Michigan, she caught fire and was totally destroyed. Succeeding her in name was a large schooner capable of carrying big cargoes of lumber, salt, coal or iron ore. Normally, her owners could quite reasonably expect her to earn a fair profit over a number of years. But again, before a fraction of their original investment had been recovered, the schooner was wrecked in a fall storm. Next to assume the promising but unlucky name was another steamer, built at Wyandotte, Michigan. The jinx was still in evidence, however, for one night in 1898, while proceeding down Lake Michigan in gusty weather, fire broke out over her boilers. The brisk wind quickly fanned the flames, and after battling the blaze ineffectually for fifteen minutes the Captain ordered the ship abandoned. From a lifeboat tossing in the seas off South Manitou Island, the chilled crew watched their ship burn to the waterline and then founder.

What happened to the first Great Lakes ship named *Phoenix* should make any man shudder at the thought of passing the name on to another craft. Nevertheless, three subsequent vessel owners did just that, much to their sorrow.

The first *Phoenix* was a combination freight and passenger steamer of some 350 tons burden, built in Cleveland and owned by the firm of Pease and Allen. She was in only her second season of operation when disaster struck. Under command of Captain B. G. Sweet, an experienced master, the *Phoenix* was steaming along on Lake Michigan on a peaceful November morning in 1847 when fire was discovered under the deck over her boilers. It spread with frightening rapidity, despite hastily organized bucket brigades and the efforts of the ship's three pumps. On board were two hundred fifty souls including one hundred sixty Hollanders, immigrants bound for new homes in Michigan and Wisconsin.

In the panic that swept the entire company, scores leaped overboard, others climbed the masts and shrouds only to plummet to their deaths when flames enveloped the entire ship. A scant few were still alive and clinging to wreckage when the steamer *Delaware* arrived on the scene two hours later. The *Delaware*, after picking up the survivors, towed the smoking hulk to shore at Sheboygan. Among the surviving Hollanders were those who later founded the city of Holland, Michigan, where even today those who died in the *Phoenix* inferno are remembered in memorial rites.

A few years later the name was given to a big open-lake tug, employed in hauling barges and scows on Lake Ontario. Residents along the Canadian shore were puzzled one night in 1863 by a bright, flickering light far out on the hazy lake. The mystery was solved days later when the newspapers reported that the tug *Phoenix* had been destroyed by fire and that the burned-out hulk had foundered in deep water. The following year a big barge carried her cargo and some of her crew to the bottom of Lake Erie in a sudden squall. Beachcombers along the tip of Long Point found plenty of wreckage, including the nameboard. It read *"Phoenix"*!

Once more the name was given to a tug, a big Detroit-owned coal burner frequently employed to tow long strings of becalmed schooners up the winding Detroit River channels into Lake St. Clair. Crews of schooners and steamers on the river were startled to see a bright glow along the Detroit waterfront one dark night. Upbound ships were hailed from the decks of downbound vessels with the warning: "A tug is afire and has been cut loose from her dock—proceed with caution!" Soon the blazing hulk came into view, being carried aimlessly by the current. Smart seamanship on the part of the upbound skippers avoided further disaster, but the fo'c'sle crews didn't need to look at her nameboard to recognize the *Phoenix!*

Occasionally a ship will be so afflicted by adversity that its name, especially if it is a family one, bestowed as a tender sentimental gesture, is abandoned in the best interests of all concerned. Such was the case of the barkentine *Jennie Graham,* built by Louis Shickluna at St. Catherines, Ontario, in 1871. In June of that year the marine editor of a Detroit paper commented that the *"Jennie Graham,* a spanking new barkentine, passed up the river on her maiden voyage, looking as trim and chipper as a yacht."

Less than a year later the *Jennie Graham* capsized in a squall on Lake Huron, about forty miles north of Port Huron. The ship floated keel up for about an hour and then turned abruptly on her side. Captain Graham, who had a substantial interest in the vessel, left the wreck, hanging on to some planking, but in a short time he and two of his crew perished of exposure. Seven crewmen were later rescued by other ships that chanced upon the floating derelict.

Towed to Port Huron, the barkentine was righted and pumped out. Two weeks later she again entered the Great Lakes trade, for that is the lot of a ship on which great hopes rest and family fortunes depend. Her existence is justified only when she is working and earning her keep for those who built her, or their heirs. A little over a year later the *Jennie Graham* was again in the news. This time she had sunk in the Welland Canal. Raised again, she continued hauling lumber, pulp wood, coal, salt, sand or whatever the charter market offered. Sinkings of sailing craft were relatively frequent affairs in the 1870's, and it was considered a rare case indeed if, after a shallow water dunking or two, a sailing ship did not qualify for a continued useful life. In fact, the *Jennie Graham* was examined the following summer by her underwriters and was classed A-1.

But the end was soon to come for the *Jennie Graham*. In April of 1880, beset by storm, again in Lake Huron, she struck a rock south of Great Duck Island, and this time she went to the bottom for good. The rock she struck is commemorated even now on Great Lakes charts as *"Jennie Graham Rock,"* a protruding chunk of granite scarcely as large as the vessel that gave it the name. Wisely, no other vessel ever ventured to leave the ways with *Jennie Graham* lettered on her nameboard. But those who officially named the rock in honor of the lost barkentine had no compunctions about using it. A jinx is for ships and names, not rocks!

The name *Dean Richmond,* with a single exception, seemed to go hand-in-hand with trouble and calamity, beginning with the schooner *Dean Richmond.* Big and sturdy, she was nevertheless driven ashore in a Lake Michigan gale, where a roaring surf reduced her to matchwood in a couple of hours. Her immediate successor, another big schooner, was launched in Cleveland in 1855 and distinguished herself the following year by departing from Milwaukee under command of Captain D. C. Pierce carrying a cargo of wheat all the way to Liverpool, England. She was later sold and her name changed, thus foiling the jinx that struck down her predecessor and was to haunt her successors.

Steam was beginning to replace sail on the lakes and the

next *Dean Richmond* was a sidewheel steamer of some 1400 tons. She followed a regular freight and passenger route to the upper lakes and was apparently headed for a profitable trading record until she caught fire in the St. Marys River, not far from the Soo. Driven ashore so that her passengers and crew might leap for safety, the grounded hulk burned and smoked for days. For years her rusting machinery became a favorite roosting spot for the gulls.

But shipowners on the lakes were slow to admit that a name in itself might carry with it a predilection of ominous happenings, and the big sidewheeler's replacement was another steamer, a propeller ship this time, one of 1432 tons and again built for heavy freight and passengers.

If the latest and last of the *Dean Richmonds* was to escape the calamities that had plagued her earlier namesakes, there was no indication of it in her yearly records of damage and claims. In 1868 she went ashore at Grand Traverse, in Lake Michigan, being freed at considerable cost to her owners. Two years later she had an engine breakdown and again towing and repair bills were high, to say nothing of the money lost while she was laid up. The following year she again went aground, on the St. Clair flats this time, the usual outrageous bills following in due course. Later the same year she caught fire while in Hay Lake, and this time it cost $135,000 to put her to rights. The next seven years were relatively free of major unpleasant events, but in 1878 she was involved in a collision with a schooner off Chicago. Her owners, because the other craft carried only sail and thus had the right of way over a steam vessel, were in due course assessed for damages. The next year she suffered extensive damage, including a stove-in gangway, in a Lake Michigan gale. Once more, the very next season, she was again in a collision off Chicago, triggering another damage claim.

For the next ten years she managed to stay clear of trouble, ten years during which her jinx apparently held her fate in abeyance, meanwhile permitting her to make the most of fair skies and calm seas in what was once the mainstay of the Great Lakes shipping industry, package freight. But tariffs were relatively unregulated and the package freight business was fast becoming a dog-eat-dog affair, with profits declining in direct ratio to the number of new ships entering the trade. Then a fortunate turn of events offered her owners an opportunity to charter her at good rates on a steady run from Buffalo to Toledo. The perils of upper lakes navigation and the uncertainties of profits were to be behind her. Ahead was a steady, good-money shuttle service that would be easy on ship and crew. And all because of what would normally be an avowed rival—a railroad!

A few years earlier, the old Toledo, St. Louis and Kansas City Railroad had decided to inaugurate a water shipping route between Buffalo and Toledo. Unlike its rivals, the road had no rail connections to Buffalo and hit upon a scheme to operate a fleet of freight boats rather than pay heavy charges to its rivals for bringing the freight as far as Toledo. From Toledo the water-borne freight would be transferred to its own rail lines, which fanned out over much of the Midwest. At the same time the railroad held that its name was far too cumbersome and announced that henceforth its popular name, except for legal purposes, would be "The Clover Leaf Route." For months then, workers were kept busy painting a big white cloverleaf on box cars, engines, tenders, gondola cars, water tanks and even the company's tools and yard buildings. In three years the new name was a household phrase all over the country, and business had boomed accordingly. They started out with two big package freighters but soon had to add others to the fleet that included the *Roanoke, John Pridgeon, A.A. Parker, Norwalk, Osceola, B. W. Blanchard* and finally the *Dean Richmond.* And like the railroad's rolling stock, they blossomed out with a big white cloverleaf on their stacks.

The *Dean Richmond* took to the run like a duck to water, and her crewmen, mostly from Toledo, were able to see their families frequently.

On the evening of October 12, 1893, the *Dean Richmond* arrived at Toledo from Buffalo on schedule and early enough for all hands to have a late dinner at home and spend the night before the fireside. Meanwhile, dock crews at the ship's Middlegrounds terminal unloaded hundreds of tons of freight consigned to midwestern points. By late evening a brisk and chilly wind had developed. The ship stirred uneasily at her moorings, hawsers creaking. In downtown Toledo homeward bound theatergoers were predicting an early winter.

Promptly at seven o'clock the following morning, fresh dock crews began loading the ship for her return trip to Buffalo. The cargo, as in the case of most package freight ships, was classified as general but included vast quantities of bagged flour, oil-meal cake, grain, feed and flour in barrels. Among the items listed on the manifest was a great load of pig zinc or lead.

As is good stowage procedure, such heavy, concentrated material is loaded first and placed far down in the ship to help serve as ballast. For several hours the laborers trundled up the loading ramps and through the side-loading gangways with hand trucks heavy with the zinc "pigs." Finally, the last of the zinc aboard, they began on the balance of the cargo. When loaded, the *Dean Richmond* was down near her winter loading marks with what should have been a profitable cargo, most of it destined for distribution in cities along the East Coast.

If any thought was given to the fact that it was Friday the thirteenth, no mention of the date as unlucky was overheard on dock or aboard ship. Cargo committed to train schedules from Buffalo could not be delayed by superstition, in any event. For that matter, if one was inclined to dire predictions, it could have been pointed out that of the crew of nineteen, one was a woman, Mrs. Betty Ellsworth, the ship's stewardess. But the old saltwater adage that a woman brings bad luck has always been generally disregarded on the Great Lakes. It has been common practice for the chief cook or steward, for example, to sign on his wife as second cook or stewardess, a tradition that exists in some lines even to this day.

About two o'clock on the afternoon of the thirteenth the loading ramps were withdrawn, the gangways bolted shut, the hawsers cast off and the order given that started the ship's big propeller thrashing half speed ahead. It was a bleak, gray day with winds gusting high. Storm warnings were already flying all along Lake Erie, but the big steamer, supposedly impervious to winds that had long since sent sailing craft scurrying for shelter, steamed slowly through the open bridges along the Maumee River. Nearly four miles of river channels lay between the Middlegrounds dock and the open lake. Even at that early hour lights were already burning in the riverfront factories as the last bridge was left astern. In the broadening reaches of Maumee Bay the first seas of the lake were beginning to make themselves felt. Captain George "Heavy Weather" Stoddard shoved the engine telegraph to "full ahead" as the ship and crew settled down to the routine of what promised to be a rough and blustery passage.

Exactly what happened during the night of the thirteenth and the grim day and night that followed must necessarily be a matter of conjecture. But, based on impressions of those who sighted her later and on the known velocity, direction and duration of the winds that raked the lake for thirty-six hours, an accurate reconstruction of events is quite possible. When, after steaming almost due north for several hours, the ship made her swing to starboard around the point of Pelee Island to put herself on the direct Buffalo course, she would have met the full fury of Lake Erie in one of her most malignant moods. The cross seas would have been pounding at her port side, possibly even breaking over her deck. All night she must have been laboring in seas that punished her brutally. Recalling that she had side-loading ports or gangways, such as had given her trouble in a Lake Michigan storm, experienced seamen shuddered to think of what must have been happening below decks as crewmen fought to bolster the gangways. In all probability her rolling and pitching caused some, if not considerable, shifting of her cargo. Normal stowage would not have sufficed in weather such as the *Dean Richmond* encountered that night and all the next day!

At four o'clock on the afternoon of the fourteenth, the lighthouse keeper at Erie, Pennsylvania, sighted the ship off that port. She seemed to be rolling excessively and making agonizingly slow recoveries, wallowing in the trough of tremendous seas from which she seemed unable to escape. She was sighted later by the steamer *Helena* and again was observed to be in trouble. But the *Helena* was having a difficult time staying afloat herself, and her captain deemed it too risky to chance closer inspection. Almost at the same time, Captain Jack Tierney of the steamer *W. H. Stevens* was watching the *Dean Richmond* through his binoculars. "She was having a devil of a time of it," he reported later. "One of her stacks was gone and even as I watched the other stack and her after spar went overboard."

Loss of steam pressure due to her second stack being swept away must have been the last straw for the harassed steamer, for she was never seen again!

Early on Sunday, October 15, a farmer living just west of Dunkirk, New York, found his beach littered with tons of wreckage, a heaving mass of flotsam that included several barrels of flour from the *Richmond*'s cargo. During the early morning, too, the body of Andrew Dodge, a cook, and that of Frank Goodyear, first mate, were dragged from the breakers. The watches of both men had stopped at 12:20! It was obvious then that the ship had foundered shortly after midnight. And since both men had perished of exposure rather than drowning, it was assumed that the crew had been able to abandon ship but could not survive the night in the cold seas and stinging wind. Later that day and the next, the rest of her crew floated restlessly ashore, singly and in twos and threes. Clover Leaf Line officials, notified by the Dunkirk harbormaster, meanwhile were rushing to the scene to identify the dead and notify anxious relatives of survivors, if any. There were none!

Mixed with the wreckage of the *Dean Richmond,* although much of it was farther west on the beach, was that of another ship, the *Wocoken,* also lost on Lake Erie with all hands. The possibility of a collision between the two storm-driven ships was ruled out, and the proximity of their wreckage deemed a curious coincidence. The *Dean Richmond* didn't need another ship to send her down. An angry Lake Erie did that—Lake Erie and the jinx that had haunted her practically since launching day!

What's in a name? Landlubbers may pose the question with impunity, but to generations of Great Lakes sailors there are always the memories and yarns about the *Queen of the Lakes,* the *Oneida, Phoenix, Racine, Jennie Graham* and the *Dean Richmond,* each name forever linked with disaster in some form, a heritage of calamity from which there was no escape.

There are other ill-omened names of course—names that were seemingly a prophecy of things certain to come—the

*Evening Star, Ada, Baltic, Albany, Calcutta, Dauntless, Emily, Java, Minch, Petrel, Sea Gull* and *Zephyr*. In every instance each was under an evil spell that brought a succession of calamities: storms, strandings, collisions and fires.

And so indeed . . . what's in a name?

# 6

⚓

# *The Clemson Is Overdue — Again!*

Already a businessman at fourteen years of age, Albert Williams knew every foot of the Lorain, Ohio, riverfront, from the stone piers at the sand dock past the tug office, shipyard, the railroad storage yards and the big coal-dumping machines all the way to the steel mill ore docks far up the winding Black River. And uptown, at Reagan's Marine Grocery, Frank Geiger's hardware store, the ship chandlery stores and any number of sailors' hangouts where his duties carried him, his bright eyes and ready smile had earned him the reputation of being a sharp, dependable lad.

Every morning he rose early to tramp his newspaper route along the river. He visited every dock and store, each watchman's shanty, and climbed aboard the ships, selling his papers from pilothouse and fo'c'sle to galley and engine room. After school he made the rounds again with the afternoon papers, finishing just in time to hurry home to dinner. The dock police used to say one could set his watch by the boy's schedule.

But there was another aspect of young Williams' business

life that, in this day before seafarer's union and hiring halls, placed him in a special category with masters and mates. Alert, watchful and friendly, he knew and was known by every sailor in town. When a vessel was short-handed he knew not only who were available but their ratings and where they were quite likely to be found. It was a simple businesslike arrangement. He merely supplied information as to the probable whereabouts of experienced sailors temporarily at liberty. The jobs were offered by the masters or mates and, if accepted, the youngster's reward for his knowledge, in the year of 1908, when this story begins, was twenty-five cents for a deckhand or coal passer, fifty cents for a wheelsman or watchman. The signing of a porter rated a quarter and, often as not, a piece of pie fresh from the galley!

That's how Albert Williams happened to meet Burt Balfour, steward on the steamer *D. M. Clemson.*

The occasion was an unhappy day in 1907 when the steward faced the grim prospect of doing double duty for a trip, his assistant having lost a bout with demon rum and the Lorain police a brief two hours before the ship was scheduled to sail. Young Williams earned Balfour's firm friendship by finding an experienced replacement in less than an hour— the steward's gratitude being expressed immediately in the form of a whole, freshly baked pie and throughout the season by giant helpings of cake, cookies and doughnuts.

Their friendship ripened during the winter of 1907–1908 when Balfour was appointed shipkeeper as the *Clemson* tied up in Lorain. It was a lonely job, made less disagreeable by the daily visits of the young newspaper merchant with the friendly smile. Cheerfully, too, he made frequent trips uptown to replenish the steward's tobacco supply, mail letters and shuttle bundles to and from the laundry. In nearly every instance his reward was a fresh pie to take home to the family.

The season of 1908 turned out to be a brisk one, and the

*Clemson,* along with the rest of the Great Lakes fleet, started early and had trips scheduled until mid-December. She loaded ore at Duluth one cold, bright November 20, slipping out of the harbor just as the sun winked down over the steep hills behind the city. Her cargo of eight thousand long tons of ore was destined for Ashtabula, nearly one thousand miles away on the south shore of Lake Erie.

The *Clemson* was far from land when the gale struck, a gale the likes of which Captain Sam Chamberlain reported he had never experienced before. This was a broad pronouncement, for only three years earlier he and his ship had met with a real howler. They had been caught far out in Lake Superior and were driven for endless hours at the mercy of the wind and the seas. When they limped into port after being "missing and presumed lost" for three days, the *Clemson* had so much water in her holds and ice on her deck that she carried a four-foot list to port.

This storm was even worse! Following seas broke over the stern, dropping tons of water on her after quarters. Her engine room skylights were smashed; cabin doors buckled and rivers of cold water coursed through the after end companionways. When Captain Chamberlain altered course to ease the danger of a flooded engine room the great rollers pounded the length of the spar deck to smother the forward deckhouses in a lather of water. Early the following morning the wind shifted suddenly, moderating the seas somewhat but bringing an awesome drop in temperature. The *Clemson* was taking green water over the bows now, and each sea left a thickening layer of ice over the entire ship. It built up on the pilothouse windows so quickly that the Captain ordered second mate Charles Woods to break out the windows with the fire ax. For the better part of two days the *Clemson* barely held steerageway until the seas calmed and a course could again be set for the Soo. She came into the locks so burdened with ice that she resembled a frosted cake in the vague shape of a ship—the kind so often fashioned by landlubber bakers to honor retiring skippers.

Captain Allen Masters, a local celebrity, had spent a lifetime on the lakes, most of it in sail, and when he retired to his home a scant quarter mile from the Soo locks he was looked on as the dean of freshwater skippers. Youngsters seeking berths and officers approaching their own commands sought and accepted his sage counsel. Widely quoted as an authority in the marine columns, he had seen generations of ships and men come and go, and his evaluation of things marine was outspoken if not infallible.

Quite a crowd had gathered at the locks, despite the weather, to see the "missing" ship lock through. Among them, surrounded by old cronies, stood Captain Masters.

"This is the second time she's gone missing," he observed thoughtfully, "and the third time is the last—it always is!"

But aboard the *Clemson* they were too busy to worry about the future. Before the ship eased past old Sailor's Encampment the crew had steamed and hacked much of the ice from the superstructure, and chief engineer McCoy had sent a man forward to put new glass in the pilothouse windows. By the time they passed Detour nearly all evidence of their bout with Lake Superior had been erased.

The *Clemson*, built at Superior, Wisconsin, in 1898, was a sturdy flush-decker just like her sister ships, the *James H. Hoyt, D. G. Kerr* and the *James H. Reed*. The *Clemson, Kerr* and *Reed* were owned and operated by A. B. Wolvin of Duluth. The *Hoyt* was owned by the Provident Steamship Company, also managed by Wolvin. They had all experienced their share of storms, but during the long winter months in Duluth, as skippers yarned before the fireside, it was Sam Chamberlain of the *Clemson* who could tell the

best stories of storms and gales and the ships and men who
lived through them.

Late but safe, the *Clemson* arrived at Ashtabula, where
dock crews went quickly to work clamming the ore cargo out
of her. After dark on the evening of November 27 she cleared
the piers light and headed for Lorain where her next cargo,
7800 tons of soft coal, waited in hopper cars on the dockside
storage tracks.

Shortly after daylight, as the empty vessel neared Lorain,
Captain Chamberlain made a personal inspection of his ship,
checking for signs of strain or damage that the stiffening effect of the heavy ore cargo might have concealed. The *Clemson* had worked heavily in the storm, as all good ships will
do and are built to do, a constant flexing and twisting to
compensate for the rising and falling seas. In the best of
ships this will sometimes cause rivets to spring, leaks to
develop. But in his long and close scrutiny of the deck plates
he found not a single crack or wavy plate. And in the cavernous cargo holds there was not a single trickle of water to
indicate rivet heads sheared off by working plates.

"She's a solid ship," he confided to Mate McLeod, "a
solid ship."

It was ten o'clock that Thanksgiving Day morning of
November 28 when the *Clemson*'s lines were made fast and
the engine order telegraph rang to "finished with engine."

Traditionally, lake docks do not work on the Thanksgiving holiday and the Lorain dock was no exception. Aboard
ships, too, under way or at the dock, it is, again by custom,
a very special day—the time when cooks and stewards present
their culinary triumphs in vast variety and quantity. It is a
day for roast turkey and chestnut dressing, giblet gravy,
mashed and sweet potatoes, roast duck and almonds, Virginia
ham with cherry and pineapple sauce, rare roast beef and

Yorkshire pudding. It is a day for celery and relish trays, cake and lemon sauce, apple and pumpkin pies, salads, cheese, fruit and coffee. No hotel could offer finer fare than a typical Thanksgiving Day dinner aboard the well-found lake vessel, and the *Clemson,* thanks to steward Burt Balfour, was one of the best "feeders" on the lakes.

Albert Williams was aboard the *Clemson* that morning with his bag of newspapers and, tracking down wondrous smells to their point of origin, found his friend basting turkeys and ducks in the ovens of the big coal range.

"Ah, lad," grinned the steward, "you'll be having dinner with us, I hope?"

"No thanks, Burt, they'll be expecting me home soon and you know how mothers are about wanting their families around them on Thanksgiving Day."

"Right-o lad, but remember that you're welcome any time."

Early on Friday the twenty-ninth, the big chute of the coal dumper rattled down, and the coal, a carload at a time, began to roar into the *Clemson's* hold. Winchmen stood by in the frosty air to shift the vessel back and forth, spreading the cargo evenly in her holds.

Down in the fo'c'sle two deckhands were packing their seabags and bidding good-bye to shipmates. They wanted no more of Lake Superior that season or any other season. Days before, when it looked as if the ship might not survive the storm and ice, they'd made a pact to quit—after the Thanksgiving Day feast!

First Mate McLeod, who paid them off, was unhappy about the whole affair.

"Now I've got to go uptown and find a couple of deckhands," he grumbled to Captain Chamberlain.

But for once Albert Williams wasn't around to tell him where a couple of unemployed sailors might be found. He was elsewhere on affairs of business, for which he has since been eternally grateful.

Near Eighth and Broadway Mate McLeod, deciding that he was not going to be too particular about the qualifications of new hands at this point in the season, spied a couple of likely-looking lads in Arthur Burkhart and James Grattan, cousins who had graduated from high school but who had been unable to find work.

"Looking for a job, boys?" called the mate. "If so, get your clothes and be at Number Two coal dumper at the foot of Fifteenth Street in an hour!"

It didn't take the boys long to decide that they wanted to become sailors, and in less than the prescribed time they were climbing the ladder to the *Clemson*'s coal-littered deck.

Meanwhile, Burt Balfour, in the throes of a temporary financial emergency, was uptown himself, trying to float a five-dollar loan. He succeeded at Frank Geiger's hardware store, proffering a new raincoat for security.

"Sure, Burt, sure," grinned Geiger, who knew the ways of a sailor and was aware that the *Clemson* probably wouldn't be back until spring, "I'll be seeing you the next trip."

Albert Williams had made the rounds of the fo'c'sle and after-deck cabins with the afternoon papers when the last car of coal rumbled down. The big chute was groaning upward, and the overflow on the ship's deck was being shoveled up by hand as second mate Woods called out the draft figures for the captain to enter in the log.

"We're drawing 17 feet, 11 inches, forward and 18 feet, 7 inches, aft."

Young Williams was going down the ladder as Mate McLeod called for a couple of hands to man the mooring hawsers.

"Never mind, Mr. McLeod," he called, "I'll cast off the lines."

"Good boy," grinned the mate, "We'll make a sailor of you yet—and I've a hunch you're a better one now than a couple of deckhands we have aboard."

When the winches clanked ahead enough to provide slack the bowline was let go, and seconds later, as the ship began to edge out into the stream, the heavy stern hawser was cast off to splash into the river and be drawn dripping to the after deck.

The *Clemson's* whistle gave one sonorous blast to signal her departure as Albert Williams stood in the gathering dusk to wave good-bye. Burt Balfour was apparently busy, as heavy smoke from the galley stovepipe attested, and the two new and green deckhands were too occupied coiling the wet hawser to notice. Only porter Hilmer Anderson, taking down the flag from the ship's after flagpole, and first assistant engineer Lee Cunningham, peering from the engine room gangway, were in a position to see and acknowledge the farewell wave.

Lights were winking on all over the dock and town when the *Clemson*, a silhouette against the blue-gray evening sky of Lake Erie, passed the harbor piers, swung west-nor'west and set her course for Southeast Shoal.

From then on her passage was a matter of time—the time she steamed past the Detroit reporting station, the time she was logged at Detour and the time, 9:30 A.M. on Sunday, December 1, when she locked through the Soo.

Strangely, two men named Chamberlain were masters of vessels locking through upbound that morning, Captain Sam Chamberlain of the *Clemson* and Captain Frank Chamberlain of the *J. J. Brown*. The *Brown* had been just astern of the *Clemson* in the same lock and had remained close through the winding upper St. Marys River channel into Whitefish Bay, their hooted passing signals to downbound vessels coming almost in unison. Unlike the *Clemson,* the

*Brown* was light, burdened only with water ballast. When they reached Whitefish Point each skipper laid his course for Duluth, the decision being largely a matter of personal preference in those days, the upbound courses permitting much more latitude than they do now. The wind was fresh, and falling barometers told of bad weather to come.

Captain Sam Chamberlain chose a southerly route while Captain Frank Chamberlain put the *J. J. Brown* on a curving northward course, far from land. Soon, in the haze of twilight on that winter day, they became known to each other only as wisps of smoke on the distant and darkening horizon.

Captain Frank Chamberlain's decision was doubtless based on the fact that in event of bad weather his ship, riding high without cargo, would be much more at the mercy of high winds and seas. Under those circumstances he wanted no part of the grim rocky south shore of Lake Superior!

Sometime after midnight the bad weather the barometers had been predicting came—came in the form of a full-blown gale, building up with such speed and intensity that shipmasters caught in it were unanimous in declaring it the worst they had ever encountered. At the time the first hurricanelike blast hit, the *Brown's* master estimated that his ship had logged some seventy-five miles after leaving Whitefish Point.

I find it hard to describe [he told an investigating board later]. It was simply the worst gale I was ever in. High out of the water as we were, every sea would seem to swamp us, breaking completely over the boat. Eventually we had to shut down our engine and let the winds blow us where they would—for 12 hours. Fortunately, we had plenty of sea room and were without cargo. I would have hated to face those seas if we were loaded!

The *Clemson*, however, was carrying her normal winter draft, the 7800 tons of coal leaving her only the allowable freeboard. She would be slow to rise to the seas, and those that struck the *Brown's* high bow and sides would have climbed aboard her, hundreds of tons of water combing her decks and hatches and smashing at her cabins. And then there was the matter of sea room. The southerly route he had chosen would not permit Captain Sam Chamberlain to let his ship be driven before the gale, even though it would in some degree lessen the buffeting she must have been taking. The shift would have involved the distinct certainty that sometime the *Clemson* would slide into the trough of the seas from which she would likely never recover . . . never have the power to swing back into the seas, bow first, which would have been her best, her only defense.

Neither could Sam Chamberlain seek shelter, for in all the miles of forbidding shoreline from Whitefish Point to Keweenaw Point there is scarcely an inlet that offers protection from a northwest gale. Only Keweenaw Point itself offers anchorage and shelter from a gale from this direction, and the *Clemson* must have been nearly a hundred miles from Keweenaw—eight hours' steaming in good weather, an eternity in such a storm in which she was now engulfed. In any event and in any direction he might turn, the master of the *Clemson* would have to assume the calculated risk of swinging broadside to the seas, and Sam Chamberlain knew the folly of such a maneuver!

The *J. J. Brown,* battered and encrusted with ice, reached Duluth some forty-eight hours late, even as her anxious owners were chartering search craft.

"The *Clemson* is overdue," they reported to the Captain.

"Little wonder," said the *Brown's* master wearily, "I doubt that a loaded vessel could have survived if she encountered anything like the wind and seas we met."

In their hillside home above the city, the family of Captain Sam Chamberlain, even after still another day had passed, would not accept the fact that disaster had overtaken the *Clemson* and her entire crew.

"Sam Chamberlain has always brought his ship home," they kept telling friends, "and he will this time!"

In the years of sailing ships delays of days, even weeks, were an unavoidable and accepted part of the shipping business. When a ship was overdue it was assumed, as was nearly always the case, that she had run afoul of bad weather or adverse winds, perhaps both, and was either anchored for days waiting for weather or tacking about trying to get back on her correct course. No alarm was felt until she became seriously overdue after other vessels in the same area made their ports. Even then there was the possibility that she had been driven into some little-traveled and lonely part of the lake to be dismasted or driven ashore, in which event she might have to wait a week or more for word of her plight to reach a port where tugs could be chartered or arrangements made for a tow by another vessel.

The coming of steam and the long steel bulk carriers have changed all that. Now the ships, their average speeds carefully calculated, operate on a schedule governed by the known number of running hours from port to port, and only ice, fog or a protracted spell of extremely bad weather stays their progress. Thus, when a steamer is overdue even for a day without the master notifying her owners, they become anxious and worried even though a gale such as the one that lashed Lake Superior that Sunday night would have delayed the largest and most powerful transatlantic liner.

But Sam Chamberlain didn't come home this time. The day the *Brown* docked safely all upbound vessels leaving the Soo locks and the downbound ships from Duluth, Superior and Two Harbors were told, "Be on the lookout for the steamer *Clemson* . . . or her wreckage." They found nothing!

At the Soo old Captain Masters, while sorrowing over the *Clemson* and her crew, experienced the doubtful gratification of a prophet whose most pessimistic predictions had come true.

"The third time is the last," he had said, "it always is!"

Captain Tom Healand of the steamer *Dundee* had been in the general vicinity of the ill-fated ship's probable position the day after the storm; when his ship docked at Ft. William he reported seeing wreckage that he assumed was from the *Clemson*, but the seas were still too high to risk an investigation. Another report had wreckage sighted on the rocky shore on the west side of Whitefish Point, but the search tugs found only a welter of shattered timbers and a battered wooden pilothouse, painted red. The *Clemson* had steel deckhouses and pilothouse and all were painted white!

After ten days the *Clemson* was still overdue, as she is today.

Many shipmasters were of the opinion that she had suffered a serious mechanical breakdown and while without power to help herself, fell into the trough of overwhelming seas. But surely, in such an event would it not take several such seas to engulf her? They would almost certainly have swept her decks clear of cabins and pilothouse, littering the seas with her wooden paneling, furniture, bodies, trunks, hatch covers, mattresses and other debris. With so many vessels searching and watching, something would have been found to indicate that the ship had been pounded to pieces by the seas.

Others hinted that in the gale the *Clemson* had encountered on her downbound trip she may have suffered severe structural damage, damage that went undetected until the wrenching and twisting of the second storm caused her to fracture plates and open her hull to the seas. But Captain

Sam Chamberlain had inspected his ship that Thanksgiving Day morning and found not so much as a sheared rivet!

The master of the *Brown*, speaking from his own experiences in the Sunday night gale, concluded that she had just "sailed under," that one or two successive seas such as had battered his ship would, in the case of a heavily laden vessel, simply have pounded her down in minutes.

Whatever happened to the *Clemson* came with such speed and cataclysmic force that there was no time to launch boats, even if that operation had been possible in seas typical of Lake Superior that night.

The career of Captain Sam Chamberlain was over as were those of twenty-two others, including the hopeful young recruits from Lorain, Arthur Burkhart and James Grattan. The Captain's career had spanned thirty years, theirs just three days!

And back in Lorain young Albert Williams was soberly pondering the fact that he had been the last person to leave the ship, giving thanks to the Almighty, too, that he hadn't been available when Mate McLeod was looking for a couple of deckhands.

In his hardware store Frank Geiger thoughtfully rolled Burt Balfour's raincoat up in paper and put in on a shelf with the penciled notation "to be held until called for."

The official search for the wreckage of the *Clemson* ended with the winter freeze-up, but when the ice melted the next spring John Cunningham of Toledo, brother of Lee Cunningham, the *Clemson*'s first assistant engineer, organized a party to search Lake Superior's south shore from Whitefish Point to the outermost tip of Keweenaw Peninsula. They found only a battered section of wooden hatch cover, which may or may not have come from the missing ship. Hatch covers were plentiful along the shore in 1908, and those of one ship look exactly like those of another.

After they retired both Frank Geiger and Albert Williams got together frequently to yarn about "the good old days." The former newspaper boy never lost his love for the ships and sailors of the Great Lakes and, at the time of his death in 1966, had accumulated a tremendous collection of ship photographs. And until the day he died Frank Geiger had Burt Balfour's raincoat, still marked "to be called for."

"You know, I've always sort of wished that I had stayed for that Thanksgiving Day dinner," Williams often mused, wistfully.

"Anyway," Geiger used to philosophize, "that old fellow at the Soo was right . . . they never come back the third time."

# 7

⚓

# *The Christmas Tree Ship*

To the wholesalers holding forth in the commission markets that dotted the area around Chicago's old Clark Street bridge, the arrival of the creaking old three-masted schooner *Rouse Simmons* was the traditional harbinger of the Christmas season.

Every year, for as long as many of them could remember, the *Rouse Simmons*, Captain Herman Schunemann owner and master, had topped off her seasonal wanderings with a big and always profitable November cargo of Christmas trees. Likewise, the annual haul spelled a fleeting era of prosperity for the denizens of the flophouses and mission dormitories of the district, for Captain Schunemann, whose thriftiness was legend, employed the derelicts to "work cargo." And though the labor was hard, it was of short du-ration—a quick way to earn drinking money for a day or two. The itinerants had a choice when they worked for the Cap-tain: they could take their pay in cash or trees. The latter course, while slightly more remunerative in the long run, involved peddling them to the home-bound crowds of office workers on distant street corners. Only those with some vestige of ambition left took the trees; mostly they grabbed their money and headed for the nearest saloon.

Dean of the men of leisure and usually accompanied by olfactory evidence of strong drink, was peg-legged and be-whiskered Claud Winters, Captain Schunemann's contact man among the derelicts. For between Claud and the Captain there existed a strange bond. Seemingly worlds apart in their respective niches in life, an unexplainable psychological reaction brought out unsuspected qualities in each. Though they cursed each other mightily and in high good humor, underneath there ran an undercurrent of understanding and sympathy.

In Claud, the Captain saw an absolutely uninhibited individual unfettered by the responsibilities that had come early in the life of Herman Schunemann. Soft-hearted and kind under his unkempt, case-hardened exterior, Claud was apparently happy and contented as the dean of the footloose legions who came and went as they pleased.

On the other hand, Claud envisioned the Captain as a fearless seaman, a rugged master on the great wastes of fresh-water where he himself might have sailed but for a leg left under a boxcar in his youth and the resultant years of discouraged and spiritless wanderings.

Captain Schunemann, who hailed from Manistique, a tiny port on the northern shore of Lake Michigan, had long since earned the reputation of being a smart operator, one who played his cards close to his vest. His long-standing feuds with tug companies and bum boat skippers over berthing charges and the prevailing rates of beef and bacon had, over the years, inspired a legend of stinginess that enlivened the gossip of dockside saloons from Buffalo to Duluth. Most of the stories were exaggerated.

Everyone agreed though, that the Captain was a great

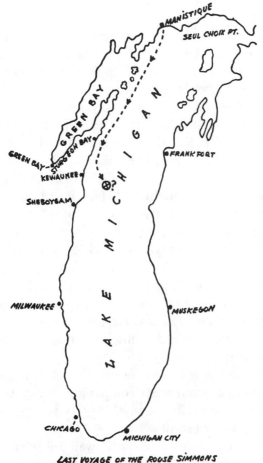

*LAST VOYAGE OF THE ROUSE SIMMONS*

sailor. They recalled the gale of '89 when the *Rouse Simmons* was the only sailing craft on Lake Michigan to escape dismasting or foundering. On another occasion he picked up the entire crew of the old lumber hooker *Cletus* when she went down in a Lake Huron storm that was threatening to send the schooner down, too. A little stubborn and headstrong perhaps, but Herman Schunemann was, without a doubt, a great sailor!

But, gruff, curt and highly conservative in money matters toward others, the Captain, in his voyages to Chicago, had displayed a perverse streak of light-hearted generosity toward the stocky, peg-legged Claud.

Once the Captain had laughingly flipped a silver dollar to him, saying, "Always keep this and you'll never be broke." Years later Claud still had the cartwheel tucked away in his ragged wallet, and only he knew the sacrifices made to keep it. Whenever they met, Claud delighted in hauling out the coin, saying, a little pridefully, "Here it is Cap . . . still as good as new and still a-yearnin' to be spent." But somehow, as the Captain insisted on paying for the drinks, the old silver dollar always managed to find its way back into the wallet.

Thus it happened that on the morning of November 27, 1913, old Claud stomped out on the fog-bound Clark Street wharf, planted his scuffed wooden peg in a convenient crack in the planking, steadied himself with his good leg and sniffed mightily.

"Layin' about a mile off the breakwater," he announced dramatically to a dozen seedy companions. "Just layin' there waitin' for the fog to lift . . . anything to save tuggin' charges, damn his tight-fisted soul!"

What Claud pretended to smell was the spiced bouquet of pine and balsam in the *Rouse Simmons'* holds, although in truth, a spice-laden barkentine from the fabled Indies could have opened her hatches to windward without penetrating the overpowering smell of creosoted piling, deceased fish and cheap whisky that encompassed the group.

His nasal powers notwithstanding, Claud's information as to the vessel's probable location on that particular morning was in an ink-stained envelope under several layers of castoff clothing. How the Captain's letters managed to reach him reflected great credit on Uncle Sam's postal workers, inasmuch as Claud's address depended a great deal on which of Chicago's fifteen-cent bed-and-bath hotels was currently extending credit.

Reach him, however, it did, with the familiar scrawl, "Expect to arrive early on 27th. Same arrangement as before." The "same arrangement," which had been in effect since 1899, was an extra ten dollars in consideration for Claud's diligent efforts in notifying wholesalers of the schooner's impending arrival and rounding up enough help sufficiently sober to walk the gangplank from spar deck to dock.

By virtue of the "usual agreement," Claud had led his motley followers to the dock fully expecting to see the familiar outlines of the schooner nosing up to the dock through the oily scum that covered the river. On the morning of the twenty-seventh, however, there was, in addition to the fog, a bitterly cold wind from the east and an intermittent smattering of snow. The busy tugs were snorting upriver with grain vessels, but no schooner was in sight!

Despite Claud's worried stomping about the dock and the prolific swearing that accompanied it, the morning wore on without sign of the aged, 180-foot schooner. As the hours passed Claud alternately cursed the Captain, the weather, the schooner and the companions who were rapidly deserting him to seek shelter in the missions.

At four o'clock the lighthouse keeper reported smoke from a distant inbound steamer but no telltale masts of a sailing craft. Cold, hungry and discouraged, Claud trudged wearily up the bridge steps. Pausing at the top, he braced himself against the wind and peered searchingly toward the distant lake. Towering seas were exploding over the breakwater, the inbound steamer was nearing the shelter of the harbor, the harbor lights winked in the dusk, but there was no distant glint of light such as might come from the masthead lamps of the *Rouse Simmons!*

Up in the blunted pine-scented hills of Schoolcraft and Mackinac counties of the upper peninsula of Michigan, the old *Rouse Simmons,* her driving master and the grim days of November, 1913, are still legend.

There is an old saying that sailors are not good businessmen, otherwise they wouldn't be sailors. Captain Herman Schunemann was an exception to the rule. In an age when steam and propellers were rapidly relegating sailing craft to the boneyards, he always managed to keep the old schooner on the move and always at a profit. A deckload of boxed apples from Green Bay to Chicago, fence posts from Manistique to Port Huron, shingles from St. Ignace to Detroit, or salt from Amherstburg to Milwaukee, it made little difference to the Captain so long as the ship earned a few honest dollars. Her canvas was old and patched, her cordage frayed and knotted and her galley perpetually understocked, but the valiant old three-sticker sailed on long after newer and bigger schooners were snaked into the lonely and polluted backwaters to rot away. Her rated carrying capacity was five hundred gross tons.

The Captain's Christmas tree haul was a seasonable but highly remunerative operation typical of his enterprising spirit. It was a choice plum to be plucked before ice and snow ended the freshwater shipping season.

When the big timber operators moved westward after denuding the peninsula's hills of the choice timber, they left behind a gold mine in five, six, seven and eight-foot stands of second growth pine and balsam. Quick to see the possibilities, Captain Schunemann set about turning nature's bounty into ready cash. The low water transportation cost and the availability of cheap labor to cut, bundle and haul the trees to his dock enabled him to undersell the Wisconsin and Minnesota growers who were obliged to ship their trees to Chicago by rail.

The season of 1913 had been a disastrous one for Great Lakes vessel operators. From November 8 to 12, the worst storm in a century had mauled the shipping lanes. Ten big freighters disappeared with all hands, and a score more lay broken and stranded on the beaches. All along the lakes the shoreline was littered with masts, lifeboats, spars, bodies and ruined cargo. Four hundred seamen perished in those four terrible days, and the lakes cities were buried under record snowfalls.

It was entirely in keeping with the shrewd Captain's character that he was able to turn the excesses of nature to his own advantage. The deep snow, reaching unprecedented depths in the tree farm areas made it impossible for men and horse-drawn rigs to get to the cutting plots. Frantic wholesalers in Chicago were already clamoring for trees, and only Herman Schunemann was in a position to deliver!

So, while shipping companies were still totaling their losses in ships and men, the Captain had every available woodsman in the bush cutting trees. A steady stream of haulers dragged the cut trees down to the trails, and horse-drawn bobsleds brought towering loads to the Schunemann dock at Thompson Harbor, just south and west of Manistique.

Part of the schooner's crew bundled the trees and tossed them into the hold where others jammed them into every available inch of space from keelson to deck beams. From bow to stern, knighthead to stern post, the aged *Rouse Simmons* was crammed with the fragrant cargo.

When the hatch planking was lashed down and most of the laborers dismissed, she was well down to the winter loading line but carried her cargo with the trim dignity and grace of a well-built ship.

But the woodsmen had worked fast and efficiently. Still piled on the dock when the hatch tarpaulins were battened down were hundreds of trees, worth nothing on the dock but representing a tidy fortune in Chicago. And the thrifty Captain must have been calculating their marketable value, for just as the cook was about to announce dinner he rounded up first mate Charles Nelson.

"Get some of the men back," he ordered, "we're going to take a deck load!"

Wearily the sailors and dock hands relayed more bundles aboard. Row upon row, they were pyramided the length of the deck. From bowsprit to stern cabin the *Rouse Simmons* sagged under her burden. So little freeboard was left that her outer bobstays were submerged. They finished trimming her by lantern light, lashing the deck load as best they could. Earlier the Captain had contemplated two trips because of the unique market conditions, but the extremely cold weather and the likelihood of an early freezup indicated that only one would be possible. But that one would probably be the most profitable the Captain had ever undertaken!

At noon on November 25, in the face of a rising gale that sent other vessels beating frantically for shelter, the *Rouse Simmons* spread her patchwork canvas to the hungry winds and swung on an east sou'east tack into the surging rollers of Lake Michigan. Split by the downward lunges of her martingale and bobstays, the mounting green seas of the open lake lathered up over her bowsprit shrouds to spend their foaming fury in the matted bulk of Christmas trees stacked under her foresail boom.

The steam tug *Burger* with the schooner *Dutch Boy* in tow had safely rounded Seul Choix Point and was rolling rails under as she neared the shelter of Manistique when Dennis

Gallagher, her master, first sighted the downbound schooner off his bow. His excited hammering on the pilothouse floor quickly brought the rest of his crew to his side.

"Mother of God, look!" he screamed above the howling of the wind. "That crazy Dutchman's going out in this, an' him with every inch of canvas up!"

Unbelievingly, they peered out the port windows between sheets of water that shot over the tug's bow to sluice the upper rails and pilothouse glass. Awestruck by the sight of the gray-sailed old schooner butting into the rising seas, they shook their heads and went wordlessly back to the steamy, clanking belly of the tug, each convinced that Captain Schunemann had taken leave of his senses!

Keeping the vessel headed east sou'east just long enough to be certain of clearing Wiggins Reef and the shoals off Point aux Barques, the Captain then swung her west sou'-west on the Chicago course.

The mounting gale, blowing west sou'west, whistled over Wisconsin, gathered new strength over the tossing wastes of Green Bay and thundered on over Lake Michigan. Rolling almost undeterred through the passages above St. Martin Island and Rock Island, the giant seas caught the *Rouse Simmons* on her starboard beam as she left the quieter waters in the lee of Point Detour and Summer Island.

Caught now in the stunning force of winds that screeched onward at sixty miles per hour, the schooner heeled far over to port as the storm-taut canvas pulled at her topmasts. Protesting, her ribs and deadwood groaned as the weight of the seas fell on her weathered deck planking and tore at her bulwarks. White water covered her port rail almost continuously while the seas boarding her over the bow hammered unceasingly at her lashed deck cargo.

Huddled in the small stern cabin and the lower deck bunks while Captain Schunemann fought the wheel, the sixteen crewmen listened to the wild, discordant shrieking of the gale as it played an agonizing symphony in the time-worn top hamper.

Above the gurgling rush of the seas they heard the brash strumming of the gale laboring at the big sticks. Wildly the wind discarded the masts and howled through the maze of shrouds, stays and lifting blocks converging near the trestle trees. Blocks, stays, wire, rope and chain, each gave out its own peculiar snarling chant audible above the anvil chorus of the mast hoops, each clanking and chattering a different eerie dirge against the masts and booms.

Below them they heard the tortured moaning of the mizzenmast laboring in her oaken steps. Forward in the hull, the fragrant cargo of pine and balsam trees deadened the sound of the joints working and whining in chorus.

Sometime during the night, as some of the sailors were checking the lashings, a tremendous sea swept over the ship. With a sodden scraping rush many of the bundled trees went over the port side, taking two sailors and the small boat for good measure.

Freed of some of her burden, the *Rouse Simmons* shook her jib stays like a punch-drunk fighter and waded into the rearing greenbacks off Porte Des Morts.

Lashed together near the wheel, whose violent thrashings now claimed their combined efforts, Captain Schunemann and first mate Nelson saw a glimmer of hope in the situation.

"We might save her now," the Captain shouted. "Give me a little daylight and by Godfrey, I'll get her into shelter at Bailey's Harbor!"

There are some who believe the Captain might have made the harbor safely but for a sly caprice of Mother Nature. Just at dawn, when the first ghostly light would have enabled the Captain to get his bearings, the wind, without abating, suddenly swung into the east and now with it came a furious snowstorm and a breathtaking drop in temperature.

The seas still swept over the gallant old schooner, but when they rolled onward they left a thin white coating of ice, a coating that thickened with each succeeding sea. By eight o'clock the *Rouse Simmons* was helpless. Her torn sails and lower rigging was a rigid formation of ice, with her ice-sheathed masts jutting up like frosted church spires. Huge knobs of ice grew alarmingly on each tackle block, cleat, lanyard and chock.

Held down by the mounting tons of ice that built up on her bobstay chains, martingale rigging and bowsprit, her bow sloughed into the surging green hills with a beaten, almost subservient spirit. The water cascading into her hold through the battered hatch covers fell upon the bundled trees, and soon water and cargo were turned, as one, into ice.

At noon on the twenty-sixth, during a temporary lull in the snowstorm, surfmen of the old United States Lifesaving Service spotted the *Rouse Simmons* from the station tower at Sturgeon Bay. She was flying distress signals and was low in the water but was apparently being driven swiftly along by the gale.

Ringing the alarm bell, the surfman ran to the tower steps and shouted down, "Three-masted schooner in distress off the ship canal!"

After a hurried conference between officers and men, it was decided that it would be impossible to catch the storm-driven ship with their small surfboat. The news was telephoned to the Kewaunee station some twenty-five miles to the south. There the lifesavers immediately launched a large surfboat and rowed outward in an attempt to intercept the distressed schooner.

For two hours they searched the heaving seas without success.

Suddenly there came another lull in the storm, and someone cried, "There she is!"

A sorry sight she was. The remnants of her top'sls flapped
furiously like a forgotten flag on a courthouse steeple, her
cordage swung in frozen knots, and the hull, burdened down
by hundreds of tons of ice, had barely enough freeboard to
keep her afloat, each rushing comber taking her down still
farther.

Desperately the lifesavers pulled toward her; but before
they could cover a fraction of the distance the smothering
blanket of snow came again, and the schooner vanished from
sight like a phantom derelict.

No living person ever saw the *Rouse Simmons* again!

There was a shortage of Christmas trees in Chicago that
year but not along the Wisconsin shore. On December 12
and frequently thereafter, commercial fishermen from Two
Rivers Point reported bitterly that they found their nets
clogged with Christmas trees—hundreds of them!

But old Claud, his faith in his friend unshaken, still insisted to all who would listen that the *Rouse Simmons* would
eventually come in. Daily he haunted the old dock under
the Clark Street bridge. Even the newspaper stories of the
bottle and note found on the beach at Sheboygan, Wisconsin, failed to discourage him.

The note had said:

Friday . . . everybody goodbye. I guess we are all through. During the night the small boat was washed overboard. Leaking
bad. Ingvald and Steve lost too. God help us.

                                        Herman Schunemann

But days passed without word from the *Rouse Simmons*.

Unnoticed by the carousing revelers in the waterfront
saloon, old Claud crept out on Christmas Eve for one last
visit to the dock. The wind whistled through the bridge's

supporting timbers, and the snow came fitfully. At midnight the wind died down and the snow fell softly in an enveloping blanket that drowned the tops of the pilings like freshly whipped meringue.

He was still there at the dock when they found him the next morning. Only his face, protected by the sagging brim of a battered hat, was free of the white coating.

Briefly, the wan sun of a Christmas morning glistened through an opening in the gray clouds as a policeman turned him over on a stretcher. A silver dollar, slipping from his stiffened fingers, dropped unseen through a crack in the planking to plunk into the oily backwaters.

"Looks like too much Christmas spirits," said the young police surgeon.

The hardened beat cop spat and grinned. "Yeah, too much Christmas spirit."

Ten years after the *Rouse Simmons* disappeared Lake Michigan yielded another and final clue. Again, it was fishermen off the Wisconsin shore who brought it to light. In their nets, along with the harvest of fish, was a battered, waterlogged wallet. It was the wallet of Captain Herman Schunemann!

# 8

⚓

## *Brothers of the Storm*

Following a blustery day of choppy seas and poor visibility
on Lake Huron, the dusk of an October afternoon in 1916
found the downbound steamers *Briton* and *Merida* approaching Port Huron. It had been an unpleasant twenty-hour passage from Detour, and ahead of them lay the night-long ordeal of navigating the winding St. Clair River, shallow and
windswept Lake St. Clair and finally the twisting Detroit
River. Both had ore consignments for Lake Erie ports of dis-
charge.

With engines checked down to the prescribed speed limit,
pilothouses "blacked out" and their red and green running
lights aglow, they began to wend their way cautiously along
the old familiar follow-the-leader course marked by buoys
and range lights. All night long, never separated by more
than a hundred yards, they snored down the channel, their
whistles sobbing fretfully in concert to acknowledge the
hooted passing signals of numerous upbound vessels.

Daybreak found them abreast of Detroit, and two hours
later, as they swung slowly to port off Bar Point to come

about on the Buffalo course, they left the protected waters
of the river to encounter the first nasty cross-seas of Lake
Erie. They were still only a half mile apart hours later when,
as they neared Pelee Passage, the wind shifted rapidly, as it
so often does on the lakes, from southwest to northeast,
quickly building up seas that caused heavy rolling and pitching.

It was time for decisions—the kind every shipmaster must
frequently make during the course of a season. Seemingly
simple decisions to those not entrusted with a master's responsibilities, they involve many people, ashore and afloat.
For a ship carrying bulk cargo, if it is to be operated efficiently and at a fair margin of profit, is necessarily attended
to by a small army of people, many of whom may never have
set foot on her deck. There are first of all the office people,
who must arrange for the correct grade of ore to be waiting
at the loading docks for prompt dispatch. Hundreds of miles
away, perhaps, officials of steel mills are establishing future
production schedules, based upon the arrival and availability
of the prescribed ore. A vessel's overhead is a costly and per-
petual item, and the cost factor is virtually the same whether
the vessel is lying idly at dock waiting for cargo or is loaded
and underway. All lake shippers subscribe to a "reporting
service" whereby, at designated points where lake traffic con-
verges, such as at Detroit and the Straits of Mackinac, shoreside observers note the time of a vessel's passing and so notify
her owners. Simple calculations then, based on the vessel's
average speed and the nautical miles to her scheduled port of
call, set in motion the facilities required to unload her
quickly and efficiently. Dock managers notify and schedule
unloading crews; tugs that are to assist the vessel to her moorings are alerted, and the railroad people have advance notice
to assure an ample supply of waiting hopper cars. Even the
firms that furnish food, linen and the necessary mechanical

and engine room supplies base their operations on a reasonably accurate estimated time of arrival.

These are all factors that a shipmaster considers when he must at last decide whether to continue or "wait for weather," as the sailors put it. First of all is his concern for the safety of the ship and crew. Secondly, and supposedly subordinate to the first, is the fact that much additional expense is incurred if unloading crews are kept idle and unproductive, let alone the continuing and relentless overhead in wages, lapsed time and fuel for his vessel. It is even more important when the vessel is operating on a charter basis with seasonal tonnage commitments. Then hours spent storm-bound in the lee of a sheltering shore or in a harbor of refuge can easily add up to extra trips to complete the charter arrangement, and this plays havoc with profits. In any event the master, and the master alone, can make the fateful decision. And who can doubt that the latter considerations have not sometimes tipped the balance of judgment?

Today it is a simple matter for a master to pick up his ship-to-shore radio-telephone to notify his owners of dangerous or doubtful weather conditions. Often as not the matter is taken out of his hands, and if the decision of the owners is to wait for better weather, they can easily notify the affected docks by telephone. But in October of 1916 few lake ships, if any, carried wireless, and the ship-to-shore radio-telephone was still a generation or more away. Each captain had to make his own decisions, based on his long experience, his knowledge of weather patterns and the particular characteristics of his ship.

That was the case on that wild October morning on Lake Erie. The Captain of the *Briton,* concluding that caution was the better part of valor, hauled his vessel to starboard, working to the lee of Pelee Island, where he prudently dropped anchor and let his ship come about to face the wind

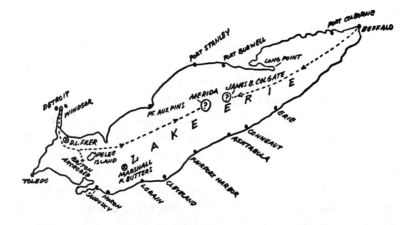

and blunted seas. On the *Merida*, however, Captain Harry L. Jones, apparently with every confidence in his ship, continued without hesitation on what was destined to be the final plotted course for him and his crew of twenty-three!

Where the *Merida* went down or the exact reasons for her loss are as much a mystery today as in the days following her disappearance, when search vessels combed the lake for her or for identifiable wreckage. Hull Number Ninety-five when she was launched in 1893 at the F. W. Wheeler and Company shipyards in Bay City, Michigan, the *Merida* was still a "young" ship by freshwater standards, only twenty-three years old. She had a keel of 360 feet, an over-all length of over 380 feet and a registered gross tonnage of 3329.

In the ordinary course of events, when a general cargo ship disappears in particularly heavy weather, the first assumption is that her cargo shifted to such a degree that all stability was lost. Then, unable to maneuver or keep her head to the seas, she would quite likely fall into the troughs, never to recover. But the *Merida* was carrying a bulk cargo of iron ore, a dense, heavy cargo—perhaps the most stable cargo a ship can carry. Lake ships have been known to roll their very keels out of water without shifting their ore cargoes; in all the history of lake shipping there is only one recorded instance of a similarly laden ship capsizing, and even there it is known that she was in collision while rolling heavily. The picture alters radically, however, if torn or ruptured hatch covers permit tons of water to join the cargo. Then there is a tremendous weight surging back and forth, a condition the master and crew would be helpless to control. Something of that nature must have overtaken and hammered down the *Merida,* for a well-constructed ship such as she was does not lack stability as long as her hatches are tight and her cargo dry. One can only assume that the towering graybeards that stalked Lake Erie that day ripped off her hatch covers and completely flooded her holds. Repairs would be out of the question and foundering would be only a matter of time. The Captain and mate in the pilothouse of the *Briton* were the last to see her—trailing a stream of black smoke as her stack and spars pitched and rolled wickedly!

The weather, instead of moderating, continued to deteriorate as the day wore on. By dusk the storm had already claimed two vessels. The old lumber hooker *Marshall F. Butters,* with a cargo of shingles and lumber for Cleveland, was beaten into submission and sank near Southeast Shoals, her crew of thirteen being rescued by two big steel steamers. The schooner *D. L. Filer* had loaded coal at Buffalo the day before and was headed for Lake Michigan when the seas beat open her seams almost within sight of the protected waters of the Detroit River. She went down in comparatively shallow water with her crew of six taking to the foremast, which promptly cracked and went by the board. Only one of the six managed to swim to the aftermast, where the Captain had taken refuge, and he perished from exhaustion and exposure before a passing steamer rescued the skipper. Still

Contestants in "the greatest steamboat race in the history of the Great Lakes." The *City of Erie,* winner, above. The *Tashmoo* below. (Chapter I)

*Photo courtesy Beryl H. Scott*

Abandoned for twenty-five years, Silver Islet looked like this in a 1909 photograph taken from the protected north side. Lake Superior had long since claimed the cribbing and fill on the unprotected south and east sides. (Chapter II) BELOW: In the distance, marked by a few trees that struggle for survival, Silver Islet looks much as it did when first seen by Thomas Marfarlane's surveying party. (Chapter II)

*Photo by Don Spavin*

Steamer *Western Reserve* which broke in two on August 30, 1882, during a summer storm on Whitefish Bay. (Chapter IV) BE-LOW: Steamer *W. H. Gilcher* which on the night of October 28, 1892, vanished from the face of Lake Michigan. (Chapter IV)

*Photo courtesy of Great Lakes Historical Society*

Whatever happened to the Steamer *D. M. Clemson* came with such speed and cataclysmic force that there was no time to launch boats. (Chapter VI) BELOW: This early photograph shows the famous and fatal Christmas tree ship, departing from a Lake Michigan dock, her canvas already up. (Chapter VII)

The steamers *James B. Colgate* (above) and *Merida,* twin victims of the storm on "Black Friday" in October, 1916, which sent them to their unknown graves on the bottom of Lake Erie. (Chapter VIII)

Built at Fort William as a minesweeper in 1918, the *Bautzen* was eventually christened the *Peary* by Donald B. MacMillan and was used by Commander Richard E. Byrd in his polar exploration by air. (Chapter XII) Below: On Thanksgiving Day, 1926, the *W. E. Fitzgerald* locks through at the Soo with an added burden of 1200 tons of ice after coming down Lake Superior in a gale. (Chapter XIII)

At the Coast Guard's "Soo Control," the movement of each vessel in the convoys through the ice is carefully charted. Communication with them is by ship-to-shore radio telephones. (Chapter XIII)

Photo by *Dwight Boyer*

*Photo by Otto Schutte*

After a long day under water, Scuba divers Andy Garcia and Manuel Martinez examine old timbers and iron works thought to be from the *Griffon*. (Chapter XIV) BELOW: Many old ships lie on the bottom where the *Griffon* is believed to have perished. Here Scuba diver Manuel Martinez examines an old wreck. (Chapter XIV)

*Photo by Otto Schutte*

the storm continued, scattering the cargo into the thundering surf.

At twelve o'clock that night still another shipmaster was to make a fateful decision, and one wonders to this day what factors and pressures prompted it. All afternoon and evening, as the gale whistled through Buffalo, the Standard Transit Company's whaleback steamer *James B. Colgate* lay under the coal dumper taking on a cargo. Built in 1892, the 308-foot *Colgate* had a registered tonnage of 1713 gross tons. One of forty-odd monitor-type vessels built by Captain Alexander McDougall, the *Colgate* had a cigar-shaped hull that, according to McDougall's theory, offered a minimum of resistance to wind and water. In actual service the spoon-shaped bow was inclined to pound heavily in a head sea. McDougall theorized that his design would in time become the prototype for lakes vessels, but its disadvantages failed to slow the development of conventional ships. Despite the low profile presented to the seas when fully loaded, the whalebacks were fairly good heavy-weather vessels, although their decks were awash in almost any kind of sea. Deckhands on a "pig boat," as the sailors called them, had a hard life, for the exposed hatches required tarpaulins the year around; and while at sea the men were constantly tightening the wedges around the bindings.

Through the dark and windy hours after sunset the dumper poured dozens of cars of coal into the *Colgate*'s holds until, when the last one was upset and the load trimmed, the twenty-four-year-old whaleback resembled a surfaced submarine. Only a few feet of her hull and of course, her cabins, were above water.

Under the circumstances Captain Walter Grashaw would have been, in the eyes of any master or sailor, fully justified in waiting for better weather as were the masters of the loaded vessels even then anchored behind the breakwall. But

Captain Grashaw was newly in command of the *Colgate* after considerable service as her mate. Like many skippers and sailors of the old school he knew that whatever delays ensue because of weather or other unforeseen developments, he and he alone is held responsible when, long after the stress of the moment is forgotten, the vessel's efficiency is measured in cold statistics of tonnage carried and time lost. At any rate, Grashaw, at 12:20 A.M. on Friday, October 20, ordered the lines slipped, backed his vessel around and, when lined up on the breakwall entrance, rang "full ahead" on the engine order telegraph!

For the balance of the night and all the next day the ship butted into the roaring seas, making little progress, sometimes barely holding steerageway. At nightfall she was approximately abeam of Long Point, only a fraction of the distance she should have covered in twenty hours. The hatch tarpaulins were already loose and hanging askew, but no man could venture on deck, let alone realign or batten down the covers. The second night of pounding was more than the *Colgate* could take. Her hatches themselves began to come apart, allowing tons of sea water to mingle with her coal cargo. Sloshing back and forth as the ship rolled, it caused her to heel perilously close to the point of no return. Then the bulkheads of her small forward deckhouse began to part, and additional tons of water crashed down into her fo'c'sle and windlass room. Bow heavy, she slogged imperceptibly onward until, at about ten o'clock, she slid down, bow first!

In the black maelstrom of wreckage and heaving seas the Captain thrashed around with the rest of his twenty-five life-jacketed crewmen. Two sailors had managed to climb aboard the ship's lone life raft, and they pulled their commander aboard. Between the hour of the ship's foundering and dawn the raft was turned over and over by the cresting seas, and when the full light of day came only the numbed Captain still clung tenaciously to the rope hand grips. All the rest of the day and the following night, nearer dead than alive, he managed to hang on, and at dawn of the second day he was sighted by the officers in the pilothouse of the carferry Marquette and Bessemer Number Two, making her daily shuttle run across Lake Erie. But for Captain Grashaw's testimony as to the last fatal hours of the *Colgate,* she too might have been a mystery ship like the *Merida.*

Days later, when the seas had calmed, search vessels systematically covered hundreds of square miles of Lake Erie on the slim chance that crewmen of the *Merida* and *Colgate* might miraculously have clambered into lifeboats torn loose as the ships went down. In midlake they found several bodies, all with lifejackets securely strapped on. This solved nothing but rather added another bizarre touch to the storm that sailors still refer to as "Black Friday," for in the cluster of still men were some with lifejackets from the *Merida* and others with the stenciled markings of the steamer *James B. Colgate.* There had been no collision between the two vessels, as Captain Grashaw's testimony bore out. But, there they were, incongruous as it may seem, crewmen from both ships, bobbing grotesquely in death as if drawn together by the common bond of their lonely trade!

The two ships are still on the bottom of Lake Erie, their locations unknown. Salvagers and treasure hunters still covet the hundreds of tons of hard coal in the *Colgate's* holds, as good today as the night she went down. And with them are the hulks of countless other victims of Lake Erie's hazards of storm, fog, ice and shoal water. Many of them, like the *Merida,* took their secrets down with them, being recorded merely as ships, big and little, of wood or steel, that set out on journeys from which they never returned.

# 9

⚓

## The Affairs of Ships and Men

It is highly unlikely that in the normal courses of their respective business or social worlds the paths of John T. Kelley and Fred Masse would have converged. Nor would Mr. Kelley have been inclined to give the names of Magnus Peterson, Andrew Miller, James Barth or James Darling more than a passing thought.

Mr. Kelley was president and manager of W. C. Richardson and Company, brokers and managers not only for their own considerable fleet, but also for that of the Owen Transit Company (of which Mr. Kelley was also president). In his Leader Building office Mr. Kelley, a prodigious worker, was usually occupied with matters of considerable importance, most of them influenced by the philosophical principles espoused by all vessel managers—that by their shrewdness and business acumen, the vessels of the fleets they manage should have easy, uncomplicated passages, capacity cargoes, fast turnaround and return to their owners a fair and just profit.

Mr. Masse, a rural mail carrier from Vermilion, Michigan, was often more concerned with the most practical method of covering his route, which, on the rugged and desolate south shore of Lake Superior, near Whitefish Point, offered challenges his uniformed brothers in the great cities could never have envisioned. To him the motto of the service: "Neither snow, nor rain, nor heat, nor gloom of night stays these couriers from the swift completion of their appointed rounds," was more than an idealistic phrase—it was a way of life.

In summer and fall his horse and buggy enabled him to cover his lonely route with dispatch. But the winters of the north country are long and hard. Temperatures often drop to forty and fifty below zero and the snow accumulates as high as a man's shoulders. In this event Mr. Masse simply strapped on his snowshoes and did the best he could. It was spring that often made Masse wonder why he had ever wanted to be a rural mail carrier. The thaws were, in their own way, as violent as the months of snow, subzero weather and great winds. Primitive roads and trails heaved up and were often clogged with pines, weary of clinging to their thin layer of soil. Melting snow left the roads and forest a quagmire that defied both horses and snowshoes. It was then that he harnessed up his dog team. And since the shoreline was still snow-covered, frozen hard and free of tumbled pines, he followed it as long as possible.

It was while beating along the shore, west of Crisp Point, on March 20, 1920, that he made a grim discovery that was to enrich him by thirty-five dollars, acquaint Mr. Kelley with the affairs of Magnus Peterson, Andrew Miller, James Barth and James Darling and begin, for Mr. Kelley, a seemingly endless ordeal of letters, claims, legal forms and depositions.

Thus, in the very fact that a discovery by one so influenced the life and times of the other, their paths did cross, however tenuous the meeting.

In any event, the trials and tribulations of Mr. Kelley and

Mr. Masse were but incidentals in a greater drama of disaster and tangled lives that had its beginning at the grain elevators of Duluth some four months earlier.

On November 6 and 7, 1919, the Owen Transit Company's 3200-ton vessel, *John Owen,* was huddled under the loading spouts of an elevator, taking on a cargo of 100,000 bushels of barley. During the season the *Owen* had carried her quota of ore and coal, but for her final voyage, trip Number Fourteen in her log, she had been chartered by the Tomlinson Company for the grain cargo, consigned to Midland, Ontario.

As loads go, the barley, although it would fill her holds, would weigh only about 2800 net tons, a light load for the *Owen.* Built in 1889 by the Detroit Dry Dock Company, she was a composite ship, all steel with the exception of her bottom, which was heavily planked. Replanked in 1916, she was considered by qualified vessel men as being in fine shape. She met all the demands of the American Bureau of Shipping, which classed her, and those of the surveyors for Smith, Davis and Company, the Buffalo firm that insured her. Statistically she was 281 feet long, had a beam of 41 feet and a depth of 20 feet. Her official number was 76818.

Loading grain in Duluth in November can be a long, cold and arduous task. It was especially so in November of 1919. Already several snowstorms had lashed the port, and incoming vessels had acquired a meringue of ice and snow on their deckhouses and rigging.

On the spar deck of the *Owen,* half-frozen deckhands were kept busy making temporary tents over the hatches and around the loading spouts to keep the grain dry. Frequently the fifty-mile-an-hour winds would send the tarpaulins whipping like bed sheets on a clothesline, and loading would be suspended until they could be retrieved and lashed down again.

Relieved at intervals, the men hurried aft for coffee and the welcome warmth of steward Magnus Peterson's galley. All too soon would come first mate Horace Fisher's call for fresh hands. As mate, Fisher was responsible for loading the vessel, keeping her trim consistent with her light cargo but at the same time maintaining sufficient draft aft to give her propellers maximum "bite" for what promised to be rough weather. It was an assignment long familiar to Fisher, and he urged his men to "step lively and let's get it over with."

It was late on the morning of November 8 when the last elevator spout spewed the end of the barley cargo into the *Owen*'s holds. With long-handled rakes the loading crew leveled it off evenly and carefully. Grain shifts easily, often disastrously, in heavy seas. At long last, it seemed an eternity to the deckhands, the hatch cover planks were replaced, covered with big tarpaulins and this harsh covering snugged down by steel locking bars around the hatch combing, the bars held tight by wedges driven in at regular intervals. At noon the *Owen* was, in all respects, ready for sea.

Over a cup of coffee in his room, Captain George E. Benham, noting a steady increase in the wind, observed to chief engineer Ira Falconer: "We'll wait another day and hope for better weather. This is a winter storage cargo anyway and another day, or even two or three, won't make much difference."

Benham and Falconer were veterans. Both had come from sailor families and had taken to the decks of ships before they were fifteen. They knew, without finding it necessary to voice their thoughts, that fighting down the length of Lake Superior lightly laden in November would be a strain on the ship and her crew. A heavy cargo of ore would have stiffened and stabilized her, but loaded with barley the *Owen* would be high out of the water, offering a broader target for the winds. It would cause her to roll and pitch and twist, putting a heavy strain on her plates, engines, rudder and steering chains. It was a time to make men, especially those who must serve on her, wonder what keeps a ship together. In the case of the *Owen* it was comforting to know that she had been enduring just such conditions for thirty years without visible harm.

Ships, even though sailors endow them with souls, are inanimate objects. They are no better than the people who design them, build them and sail them. If they have long lives it is because the men who design them know intimately the stresses and strains, in all weather, they are likely to encounter in the service they are built for. The builders, too, if they are good builders, know what a ship must have to last. There can be no "hedging" on a ship's materials or specifications, even if such skulduggery should escape the sharp eyes of the surveyors from the firms that insure and class her.

But however well a ship is designed and no matter how carefully it is permitted to grow from keel to mast tip, a large measure of her success, if indeed she does enjoy success, is then up to the people who sail her—the mates who supervise her loading, the engineers who care for her machinery, the humble watchmen who peer ahead for danger, the firemen who keep her steam pressure up and the captain who charts her course, keeps her from shoals, nurses her through the channels and who instinctively protects her from all manner of harm.

This then, primarily, is the story of people and a single storm-wracked month. The month was that tragic November of 1919. The people are those of the *John Owen,* the *Myron* and the *H. E. Runnels,* particularly those of the *John Owen.* These are the people who lay snug in their bunks throughout the night of November 10 while the restless harbor waters, excited by the tenacious winds, caused the ship's hawsers to squeak mightily in protest.

They were a strangely assorted lot, the men of the *John Owen,* though in all truth the crew was probably typical of a vast majority of ships plying the Great Lakes in 1919. They were a mixture of sober, reliable hands, usually the career men in the pilothouses and engine rooms and the restless, roving itinerants who for the most part made up the deck and "black hole" gangs of firemen and coal passers.

It was the black gangs that created most of the activity in the hiring halls. During the course of a season a fireman or coal passer might serve on six or eight vessels. The hard physical labor, the terrible heat of the boiler rooms and the low prevaling wages (the *John Owen's* rate was $100 a month for firemen, $70 for coal passers) were things that could be forgotten for a few hours in a waterfront bar. And if a man dallied overlong with John Barleycorn and missed his ship the loss was not great, either for the man or the ship. A phone call to the nearest hiring hall could replace him in short order even though similar circumstances had probably made the replacement available. He, too, might last only to the first unloading port after pay day, but here other men of like disposition were waiting to "ship out" again, pockets empty and stomachs usually begging for food.

Often those of the black gangs were men without responsibilities or with reasons for wanting to forget them. Many had long since cut all ties with kith and kin and signed the articles with whatever name came to mind. Theirs was not a happy lot, and it is little wonder that the crew lists of many vessels contained inaccuracies that were no fault of the owners. Vessel owners sought to stabilize their officer personnel by offering bonuses for a full season of service, but the offer was not extended to those in the lowly capacities.

And again in truth, it is doubtful if it would have had any effect.

The crew list of the *John Owen* on October 28 numbered twenty-two, about her normal complement. One was a woman, Emma Peterson, wife of steward Magnus Peterson. Two were relative newcomers. On October 12, second assistant engineer Urban Britz, aboard since April 10, was forced to leave because of illness. His place was taken by William J. Reilley, who signed on the next day. On October 27 a man who signed on as Andy Miller began work as a watchman.

Between October 28 and the night of November 10, as the *Owen* "waited for weather," all six of her black gang had, for devious reasons, gone astray. Had they been queried as to their motives, the questioner would probably have received a variety of answers, none of which would have held up as valid or just causes. In any event, firemen David Larson, John Kuloviaz and Horace Rody, along with coal passers Harry Hallrom, Oren Wukely and Pat Murry simply "went ashore." Quickly, as a matter of course, they were replaced with men who signed on, on November 8, as August Armany, Bennett Jensen, Theodore Clark, James Darling, James Barth and Tony Deveno. And since their jobs required little more than the brawn to fire the boilers and to shuttle coal from the bunkers to the boiler room plates, they probably fitted into the ship's company as well as any six who might at the moment have been available. Like the rest of the crew, they stowed their gear, stood their watches the night of the tenth, drank the good coffee brewed by Emma Peterson and took their "sack time" on schedule.

All that night the wind continued to howl out of the northwest as it had for days. It swept down the mountain at Duluth's back door, rattled windows, blew out street lights and whipped the harbor into whitecaps. In the southern reaches of the harbor the ships tied up at the ore docks were hidden in a red dust storm as the wind shrieked through the towering loading pockets and over the hopper cars, literally deluging the ships below with powdery red ore dust. The *John Owen,* although partially protected by the high grain elevator, had extra hawsers out, and they were watched carefully throughout the long night.

The storm was still hammering Duluth the morning of the eleventh, although Captain Benham advanced the opinion that it would "blow itself out" before noon. As a matter of fact the force of the winds did seem to diminish as the morning wore on, and at noon he gave the order to "single up" on the lines, preparatory to sailing. Slowly the heavy hawsers, stiff with ice, were brought aboard, leaving only a single line fore and aft. Second mate Evans then waved the deck crew aboard and, when the last man was on deck, signaled the elevator dock crew to cast off the remaining two lines. The *John Owen,* a plume of steam curling from her whistle, hooted twice, backed into the channel, swung to starboard and headed out under the aerial bridge and through the ship canal.

If Captain Benham (he liked to be called "Ed") had any last-moment doubts about his ability as a weather prognosticator it was too late for what the politicians now call "an agonizing reappraisal."

Out on Lake Superior, where the leaden skies almost seemed to touch the seas, the wind increased in intensity, as if the morning lull had been merely for the purpose of luring trusting shipmasters from their snug anchorages.

The *John Owen* was committed now, and the great following seas that had been a-building for days left no doubt as to the course she must follow. There could be no turning back. This would require Captain Benham to put his ship in the trough of those murderous seas. Considering the

*Owen's* modest indicated horsepower of 975, it is improbable
that he could have successfully completed the turn. More
likely she would have stayed there in the deadly valleys
where she would have broached to and been overwhelmed
in moments. Another factor was the cargo. A wise skipper
treats grain with the courtesy he would accord a wealthy
maiden aunt with rheumatism. In the trough of the seas the
*John Owen* would have rolled her very belly out of the
water, and a fatal shifting of the cargo would not have been
a mere possibility, it would have been as certain as death and
taxes.

No, apparently Captain Benham never considered turning back, for the *John Owen*, black smoke pouring from her
stack, steamed on down Lake Superior, following the well-
known downbound steamer track that would keep her well
off Devil's Island. Once past the entire Apostle Islands group
he would haul her slightly to starboard for the long, bitter
and stormy course that would bring her off Copper Harbor
and Keweenaw Point. Here, if the situation seemed perilous, he could steer between the point and Gull Rock Light
to seek sheltered waters behind the point. Generations of
shipmasters have sought the same shelter in hard west and
northwest gales, even as they do today.

It is known by reports of ships that sighted her that the
*John Owen* steamed past Keweenaw Point without seeking
shelter. This fact alone would indicate either that the passage, while rough, was typical of any November voyage on
Lake Superior or that Captain Benham did not care to risk
his ship by turning her broadside to the seas while rounding the point, thus subjecting her to more punishment and
the possibility of a shifting cargo.

The *John Owen* was, in fact, sighted twice and seemed in
no worse or better shape than the vessels that later reported
seeing her.

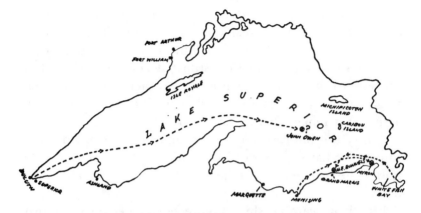

But at the Soo locks, where in due time every downbound vessel must lock through if she is to complete her voyage to the lower lakes, the *John Owen* failed to appear. For a time this was no cause for alarm, for it was common practice in such weather as Lake Superior had been dishing up for a shipmaster to seek some place of refuge and "wait for weather." This was considered very probable in the case of the *Owen* for, being light loaded, she would be more at the mercy of the gale than a ship down to her winter marks with ore.

Ship reporters at the Soo and at other points along the great inland seas forward vessel passage information to the shipping companies at regular intervals. It is an important service, on which the owners or charterers base shoreside scheduling of unloading, fueling, provisioning or any repairs that might be required. If the prescribed dock is difficult to "make," tugs are arranged for, and if the cargo is to be unloaded directly into ore trains, the railroad must have a supply of cars on hand, working crews available and numerous other details attended to. The owner's dispatcher or vessel manager, when notified, for example, that one of his vessels has just cleared Escanaba, Michigan, with a cargo of ore consigned to Conneaut, Ohio, knows almost to the minute when the ship may be expected to poke her bow around the Conneaut breakwater. Fog in the Straits of Mackinac or adverse winds on Lake Huron or Lake Erie may require an adjustment on the estimated time of arrival, but the shrewd dispatcher, listening to weather reports and getting additional information from reporting stations, can still arrive at a remarkably accurate docking time.

Today the information is even more complete, since the shipmaster has merely to pick up his ship-to-shore phone to notify the dispatcher that he will "be off the breakwall at 8 A.M."

But there were no ship-to-shore telephones on the Great Lakes in 1919, and the ship reporters at half a dozen points along the lakes were the owner's only source of information on the progress of his vessels.

Advised by wire of sailings from Duluth, Superior, Two Harbors and the south ore ports, the Soo ship reporters, familiar with the speed of every ship, knew precisely how long each, considering the prevailing weather, should take coming down Lake Superior.

There were, that November of 1919, many ships, upbound and downbound, running considerably behind schedule. Some upbound steamers had not even attempted to lock through but lay at anchor in the lower St. Marys, where good "holding ground" provided safe and protected anchorages. They lay there, a score of them, their high masts sticking up like fence pickets above the green pines along the shore.

Consequently no immediate concern was felt when the *John Owen* became overdue. But when other vessels that had departed Duluth after her made fast to the lock walls two to three days late with no sighting of the tardy ship, action was taken. From his office in Cleveland, John T. Kelley wired Duluth, checking again on the *Owen*'s departure time and asking if the Hutchinson Company, her charterers, had received any word.

From Duluth, on November 15, came the reply, by wire:

Message received. Have talked with masters all ships arriving Ashland, Two Harbors and Duluth. None of them have seen anything of *John Owen* with exception of Captain steamer *Howard Shaw* which arrived Two Harbors nine yesterday morning. He reported passing *John Owen* ten miles east of Stannard Rock at three o'clock Wednesday afternoon. At that time wind was fresh westerly, increased to gale shortly after passing *Owen*.

Two days later, by letter, came further information from Duluth:

We acknowledge receipt of your letter of the 15th, and note that at that time you had not received any news of the Str. *John Owen*. We talked to Master of the Str. *Panay*, which arrived here Saturday night. He reports having passed the Str. *John Owen* off Manitou Island about eight o'clock Wednesday morning. At that time the wind was southwest, and the *Owen* was making good weather of it. Shortly after passing the *Owen*, the Captain of the *Panay* states that the wind shifted around to the west, and blew very hard with snow. He thought that perhaps the *Owen* might be down far enough when the wind struck her so that she could round-to and head into it, and perhaps be able to get under the point.

The weather on the sixteenth was still wild, but shipmasters arriving at Duluth and the Soo were now reporting sighting considerable wreckage in or near the steamer tracks. The seas were too high to permit inspection, but one captain claimed to have sighted what looked like a battered pilothouse. Another said he saw a body, still being supported by a life jacket.

Despite weather that would have driven a sea lion to shelter, Captain Frank Root of the Great Lakes Towing

Company dispatched the tugs *Alabama* and *Iowa* to search the area thoroughly. Battered and badly iced up, they spent sixty terrible hours looking for the wreckage—and finding it. In a welter of shattered woodwork, broken chairs, boxes and the sad debris left by almost any foundering vessel they recovered one side of a pilothouse. At the top, precisely where it should have been, was a ship's nameboard. It said *"John Owen"*!

In the weeks that followed John T. Kelley was submerged in the paperwork that goes hand in hand in any ship tragedy. There came to his office all manner of legal documents, depositions, insurance claims for verification and many letters from the bereaved relatives of the crew. Some of the latter were callous and cold, coming from those who sought only whatever money the unfortunate sailor had due him when the ship went down. Others mentioned personal problems, the hopes and ambitions of the dead and inquired if the *John Owen* would be raised and the bodies recovered.

Being a practical man, however, Mr. Kelley was aware, and made the fact known, that thirty-year-old steamers are not raised from such depths as are found in Lake Superior even if the wreck can be located (which was highly unlikely), and even for such a noble purpose as retrieving the bodies of her people.

In due time Mr. Kelley saw that all relatives were notified, paid the wages and season bonuses due and tucked the receipts for same safely away in the file marked "Wreck of the *John Owen*." It would seem that the case history of the steamer *John Owen* was being brought neatly to a close or as neatly as such dismal matters can be disposed of.

But in the course of correspondence with the bereaved, Mr. Kelley had learned much of the men who shipped aboard his steamer as she lay loading grain in Duluth, much more than he would have known had she, as a matter of course, completed her scheduled trip to Midland, Ontario.

The crew of the *John Owen* included men who, for reasons of their own, had signed on with whatever name seemed expedient at the time. As a matter of fact there were three.

Watchman Andy Miller, who signed on the ship on October 27, used the name because, as his father later explained from Buffalo, "it was easier to pronounce than his real name, which was Andrew Rupprecht."

The other two were among those who shipped on through the Lake Carriers' Association hiring hall to replace the six who took French leave while the ship lay at the elevator. The man who signed on as James Barth, coal passer, it developed, was not James Barth at all. Again from Buffalo, a saddened father reported that "His real name was James Lake, but he sometimes used the name of James Barth, Miles Murphy or other aliases."

Young James Darling, or so he signed his name when he got his job as coal passer, was in reality Clyde Ralph Stalling, of Bellevue, Ohio. His mother explained that the alias was used because she and her husband had objected strenuously to his sailing.

Things were gradually being straightened out, and Mr. Kelley was beginning to think the matter about settled when, on March 22, 1920, as a result of mail carrier Fred Masse's discovery, he received a wire from A. F. Glaza, keeper of Coast Guard Station 283, at Crisp Point, on the forbidding south shore of Lake Superior. It said:

Have taken charge of body bearing identification card signed W. J. Reilley life belt marked *John Owen* found frozen in ice Sunday three miles west on point fifty miles from railroad and nearest undertaker have notified Lake Carriers Assn and requested further instructions.

Consulting his crew list, Mr. Kelley discovered that William J. Reilley of Cleveland had signed on the *John Owen* as second assistant engineer on October 13, replacing Urban Britz, who left the ship because of illness.

Lucky Mr. Britz was still alive and had already received a proportionate share of his season bonus, in his case $125.

The grim tasks and details associated with Great Lakes tragedies, following the disbursal of the moneys due the unfortunates, in those days were largely the responsibility of the Lake Carriers' Association, an industry group representing the major ship operators. In particular the painful duties fell to the association's capable long-time secretary and treasurer, George A. Marr.

Taking charge of the situation, Marr wired keeper Glaza:

Will wire soon as possible regarding body of William Reilley. In meantime please advise condition of same.

Replied Glaza:

Body of William Reilley incased in ice. Keeping it now at station. Will keep it so until taken care of by undertaker. Weather warm.

Wired back Marr:

If body of Wm. Reilley can be prepared for shipment at reasonable expense family would like to have it shipped to Cleveland. We will guarantee a reasonable amount for such expense. Would like information as to cost before final action. In meantime please have body given good care by undertaker.

From Glaza:

Explained case to undertaker Vanderhook at Soo. Requested he come and take body and to wire me estimate cost. He did not do so and replies bring body to Eckerman nearest railroad point fifty. Impossible to get team. Roads impassable. Spring breakup. Body prepared for burial here to best of my ability. Recommend he be buried here under these circumstances. Letter follows answer.

Reply from Marr:

We agree with you that the only reasonable action under the circumstances is to bury Mr. Reilley's body locally. Would like to give as good burial as your facilities permit and have body laid in Catholic cemetery if one is accessible with Catholic burial rites if possible. We will bear expenses.

Later, by letter, keeper Glaza reported:

Having continuing warm weather, it was deemed impractical to hold body longer, decided it was best to bury same at once. The burial ground here contains several graves but it is of no special creed. Accordingly, at 1 P.M. Mr. Reilley was buried with Catholic Burial Rites held by Keeper and crew to the best of their ability, most of us being of the Catholic religion were not familiar with other burial rites, also decided from the name that the deceased must have been a Catholic. The grave will be given the best possible care.

Later, in reply to another query by Marr, keeper Glaza replied:

Referring to the reward of $25 offered by W. C. Richardson & Co, agents, for the recovery of the body of any member of the crew of the Str. *John Owen,* personally I consider Mr. Fred Masse of Vermilion, Michigan, who discovered the body entitled to it. Mr. Masse same as myself is a married man with a family, and with these days of High Cost of Living, could make excellent use of it. Possibly you can take the matter up with the above named company. . . . Found it necessary to engage Mr. Masse's dog team for this purpose and consider his and the dogs' service worth at least $10.00.

Hence, Mr. Fred Masse, rural mail carrier, was $35 richer.

He was, in fact, far richer than the late Mr. Reilley had been at the time of his death. Keeper Glaza, listing his belongings, reported the following:

Identification card Lake Carriers' Assn. dated July 30, 1919 for
Str. *W. H. Donner*. Identification card Lake Carriers' Assn. dated
Oct. 12, 1919, for Str. *John Owen*. One memorandum slip
showing payment of 33 days wages by Mahoning Steamship Company covering period from July 30, 1919 to Sept. 1, noon, 1919.
One 25¢ piece, two dimes, two nickels in silver money. Seven
short pieces of lead pencils, short piece of hair comb.

Four months later Mr. Marr was busy again at the most
distasteful aspect of his many-faceted job. His actions followed a wire from one Frank Bishop at Sault Ste. Marie,
Ontario. It said, briefly:

Three bodies found on Parisian Island off steamer *John Owen*.
Two have been buried, one to bury. I have two insurance
policies and papers belonging to Peterson the steward. What
shall I do. Cable at once.

A minimum of correspondence was involved in the grim
business on the shore of Parisian Island. It was duly reported by the finder that one body bore a gold signet ring
with the initials "L. R." or "A. R."

In the course of time Mr. Frank Bishop received seventy-
five dollars for his discovery, and Mr. Marr was put to the
trouble of writing Mr. Kelley again:

"With reference to a body having a signet ring, with
initials 'L. R.' or 'A. R.,' would say that there is no L. R.
listed in the crew of the *John Owen* but there was the man
known to us as Andy Miller, whose correct name is Andy
Rupprecht."

And so, in all probability, the man who preferred to be
known as Andy Miller lies in that lonely grave on the loneli-
est of islands, where the cries of the gulls and the hooting of
distant steamboat whistles blend in a continuing requiem
for the lost *John Owen* and her crew.

All in all, November of 1919 proved to be one of the most

disastrous months in Lake Superior history. At the same time that the *John Owen* was losing her battle for survival, or perhaps even after she had slipped beneath the thundering waves that tormented her, another ship was being hammered into matchwood not many miles away. She was the *H. E. Runnels*, a twenty-six-year-old lumber hooker who seemingly carried herself with the subservient grace of an old family retainer with whom fate had dealt unkindly.

The *Runnels'* job was simply to carry lumber, as much as possible and as efficiently as possible. Usually it filled her holds and was piled on her deck as high as her pilothouse. Usually too, she towed a similarly laden barge, sometimes two. It was a slow, grinding task, shuttling between the lumber ports along Superior's shores and the mushrooming cities along Lake Erie. Many of the houses and buildings in Buffalo, Erie and Cleveland had been built of lumber she hauled those perilous miles between the upper and lower lakes. But this time it was different. As she locked through the Soo, upbound, she was loaded with nearly a thousand tons of soft coal and towed no barge. Barging on Lake Superior in November was a risky, often fatal operation. So this time the *Runnels* was paying her way with the coal cargo but would return with her familiar burden.

While she steamed outward in the protected waters of the upper St. Marys River on the morning of November 10, her fifteen people were going about their business of eating breakfast, changing watches and doing the routine chores that require frequent attention even on a vessel only 178 feet long. Her Port Huron builders had done their work well, and her 375-horsepower engine drove her at a steady, if unspectacular, pace. She had no wireless, and her people could not have known of the severity of the great storm that had been a-building for days out on Lake Superior.

One look at the battered, ice-laden freighters that rounded

Whitefish Point and snored thankfully down the sheltered river should have been enough. There is no record of any having passed along a word of warning, and if they did they were ignored. It is incomprehensible, in the face of such evidence of extremely heavy weather, that the master of the lumber hooker did not drop anchor, as bigger and better ships did, to wait for better weather.

His first awareness of the enormity of the seas came, apparently, as soon as his ship drew abreast of Whitefish Point to meet the first of the thundering graybeards that came romping unchecked over four hundred miles of water.

The great heaving seas boarded her, every one of them—charging over her fo'c'sle with the enthusiasm of playful St. Bernard pups and lavishing their affections over her decks and deckhouses. And like the untrained children of unwelcome guests taking liberties with the property of their hosts, they left their mark in the form of ice rather than sticky fingerprints. The first rimming of ice, from where the spume laced her spars to the wide deck and heavy, solid rails, grew and grew, simply because no man could venture on deck to do anything about it. The caking grew heavier with every sluicing she absorbed until the "icing" was a foot thick.

When freed of her deckload and unhindered by a barge, even though her hold might be full, the *Runnels* was inclined to display an attitude of jauntiness in any sort of seaway, rising quickly and easily with each sea and meeting the next with the devil-may-care air of a knight about to enter the jousting arena with the full knowledge that his lady fair is in the audience. But now, all too suddenly, it was different. With a hundred tons of ice on her decks and superstructure she dug deeper into the oncoming seas, rose more slowly to their upward surge and threw still more water aloft. Normally she was considered somewhat lively, answering her helm with no hesitation or reluctance. Now, with the accumulated burden of ice, she was inclined to fall off to one side or another, becoming increasingly tender and topheavy. She displayed every indication of unbearable weariness, like a tired old lady asking nothing more than to be permitted to dive into one of the big seas and keep on going down to a final peace.

Night came and still another day, with the *Runnels* somehow miraculously afloat. Down below the black gang was keeping up steam and the trusty old engine thumped out its steady symphony. But the sturdy old planking and creaking frames were taking a twisting and pounding such as they had never endured before. Caulking was working loose, and each sea found a hundred openings that had not been there the day before. The pumps were running continuously but were steadily falling behind on the demands made of them.

The *Runnels* was bound the length of Lake Superior, but her Captain was now aware that this was beyond the realm of possibility. Unless he found a refuge from the murderous seas his ship would likely never make any port.

Harbors of refuge on the south shore of Lake Superior are few and far between. In the long miles of open water between Whitefish and Keweenaw points there were only two places where a ship sore beset could safely anchor. Grand Island offered quiet waters in its lee, in the narrow passage between Sand Point and Trout Point, the normal channel for vessels making the port of Munising. Other than that there was only the small harbor at the village of Grand Marais, and the approach here was open and exposed.

In any event Grand Marais was the nearest, and the *Runnels'* helm swung sluggishly to port. This subjected her to even more twisting and working, but there was really little choice. She was going to perish anyway, and there was always the chance, however slight, that she might stay afloat long enough to make her plight known to the Grand Marais lifesaving station. The *Runnels* was now literally an iceberg with

motive power. Her crew could not abandon her, for the lifeboats were part of a huge block of ice under which were her
after cabins. The water in her hold and engine room rose
higher every hour, creating clouds of steam in the stokehold
every time it sloshed against her boilers and grates.

Shortly before daybreak on the third day out of the Soo
the old lumber hooker went aground on rocks just east of the
Grand Marais harbor piers. Fishermen spotted her at dawn
and quickly ran to the lifesaving station to report the wreck.
She was already beginning to break up, and on shore the
gathering crowd could hear an ominous, steady booming, like
distant cannon fire, as the seas exploded over her. Already
her fires were out, and her soft coal cargo was spewing from
between her wracked planking, turning the roaring surf black
and building up a bonanza that warmed the shacks of the
fishermen for years.

The deeds of the men of the Coast Guard lifesaving stations
often go unsung despite many instances of almost unbeliev-
able bravery in which many men lose their lives. Their work
that dark and stormy morning at Grand Marais must surely
rank as one of their finest hours. With only their little thirty-
foot surfboat and in temperatures that turned the flying spray
into ice the instant it touched them, they battled their way to
the lee side of the stricken *Runnels*. Four times they made
the trip, against incredible odds, to take every man jack off
the ship.

By midafternoon the *Runnels* had completely broken up,
her timbers and planking grinding furiously in the wild
surf. There are buildings still standing at Grand Marais
built partly from the wreckage of the *Runnels*.

News of the wreck and the heroic work of the lifesavers
was still the main topic of conversation a few days later as
another old lumber hooker lay at her dock at Munising taking on cargo. She was the *Myron,* eight feet longer than the

*Runnels* but five years older. But despite the traditionally intemperate weather of November she was still towing her barge, the *Miztec*. The barges in the lumber hauling trade were big old schooners, vessels that, on their own, could not compete with steam. Nonetheless, divested of their masts and running gear and towed by hookers such as the *Myron*, they were highly profitable and carried surprising cargoes.

The *Myron*, for example, could carry nearly 700,000 feet. This included all she could stuff in her hold and stack on her deck. The longer *Miztec*, unencumbered with smoke stack, stays, rigging and housing for a large crew, could take on twice as much. What's more, it took a crew of eighteen to manage the steamer, only seven on the tow barge.

The weather on Lake Superior had moderated somewhat since the *Runnels* "went on" at Grand Marais, and Captain Walter Neale of the *Myron* apparently thought it was about as good as could be expected for the balance of the navigation season. Shortly after daybreak, on November 22, the *Myron* eased away from her dock. The *Miztec*, reluctant at first, soon followed suit and like a well trained dog obediently kept her stem in the *Myron*'s wake. Once through the channel and beyond Grand Island, with Michigan's famous Pictured Rocks making a stirring panorama off to starboard, the towline was played out, putting a good three hundred feet between the steamer and her consort.

It was the final trip of the year, and the routine would have been relatively simple under ordinary circumstances; just a matter of hauling her barge, handing her over to the tugs that would chivvy her through the locks at the Soo, retrieving her again and guiding her skillfully through the winding lower St. Marys River with shortened towline, playing the line out again for the long haul the length of Lake Huron. She would shorten up again at Port Huron, while mothering her down the St. Clair and Detroit rivers and finally, lengthening the line again, pull her the full length of Lake Erie to Buffalo. It was an old story for the *Myron*. She had been doing it ten or twelve times a year for thirty-one years without undue trouble.

But quickly the circumstances stopped being ordinary. The two vessels had scarcely squared away for the haul to Whitefish Point when things started to go wrong. The weather began to deteriorate swiftly, and at times the snow was so heavy the watchmen on the *Myron* couldn't see the barge. They slogged along for several hours with only the taut, squeaking towline assuring them that the old *Miztec* was still keeping her company. Conditions topside were bad enough and getting worse when Captain Neale received evil tidings from below. The *Myron*'s engineer sent a fireman to the pilothouse to report that the ship was taking water. They could hear and see it surging under the boiler room grating and around the engine's bedplates!

By now the wind was whistling along at thirty knots from the northwest and apparently increasing, judging from the seas that were beginning to clamber aboard with frightening regularity.

Already beset with a harvest of ominous events that at some time come to every shipmaster, Captain Neale also noted that the temperature had dropped sharply, and ice, the dreaded ice, was beginning to build up, not only on the *Myron*'s hull and superstructure, but on the deck cargo.

A ship designed for a specific service, as the *Myron* was laid down for the lumber trade, has certain stabilizing factors inherent in her very structure. A lumber hooker, in addition to towing her barge, or sometimes two, must carry a deck load to pay her way. Thus, a load of lumber that would render another type of ship dangerously topheavy would not seriously affect the hooker's stability. But these stability factors do not include the addition of many tons of ice, and the

*Myron's* deck load was beginning to accumulate ice rapidly; before long that ice would be the determining factor in her survival. This consideration must have weighed heavily in the mind of Captain Neale as he agonizingly took inventory of the factors that would figure in a decision he felt should be made soon. He ordered the chief engineer to keep the steam pressure as high as possible.

But the modest boilers of the *Myron* could produce just so much steam, and much of what was available had to be used to keep the pumps working at their capacity, which was also modest. Slowly and inevitably the water rose until, as the vessel rolled, jets squirted up between the gratings, hissing in the hot ashes and filling the boiler and engine room with nauseous fumes. Again a fireman carried the word of the deteriorating conditions to the pilothouse.

The plight of the black gang crystallized the decision Captain Neale had to make. With her barge the *Myron's* present speed was three or four knots. Figuring carefully, Captain Neale calculated that without the barge he might possibly coax his vessel around Whitefish Point where, once in its lee, he might set about the business of pumping his ship free of water, hacking off the accumulated ice and, if necessary, jettisoning the deck cargo. He could even beach her should corrective measures fail, at least saving the lives of his people. Leaving a powerless barge and its crew at the mercy of what was now a full whistling gale was a decision no shipmaster would relish. But poor Captain Neale had no choice.

Strangely though, lake history has proved that the helpless barges cast adrift from their steamers had often fared better, when they had sea room and were untethered, than the steamers themselves. The ill-fated *Mataafa,* with her barge *Nasmyth,* was a typical example. Caught by a vicious gale shortly after leaving Duluth, the Captain of the *Mataafa* had turned to seek the shelter of the harbor again but in the tremendous seas had, in desperation, ordered the towline cut. The *Mataafa* was wrecked at the harbor mouth with many of her crew freezing to death in her after cabins and ventilators. But the old *Nasmyth*, presumed lost with all hands, was found by searchers, riding comfortably to her anchors. She had been through a terrible ordeal, but the ship and every man aboard her were safe.

Captain Neale signaled the barge that he was cutting the towline, knowing in advance that the captain of the *Miztec* would drop his anchors and permit the barge to swing around into the wind. But would the anchors hold? The bottom of the exposed side of Whitefish Point is rocky and not considered good holding ground. But again, there was no choice if the *Myron* was to have a chance to survive.

Now came a new witness to the race for Whitefish Point. Interlake Steamship's big ore freighter *Adriatic,* downbound and making heavy weather of it herself, was on a course that would converge with that of the *Myron.* Her skipper, too, was of a mind to slip behind the point until the gale moderated, but he could not ignore the plight of the little lumber hooker.

The *Myron,* making better time now that her barge no longer dragged astern, was still in desperate straits. Indeed, even as those in the *Adriatic*'s pilothouse watched, they saw short but continual puffs of steam coming from her whistle and the crewmen clustering near her boats. Snow squalls would obliterate the scene for moments, like a stage curtain dropping on the grisly last act of a tragedy. Then suddenly, the snow would be gone and there again was the *Myron* in her death throes. The *Adriatic* maneuvered close to break the sweep of the seas, but she was heavily laden with ore and the bottom was rapidly shallowing out.

The *Myron*'s lumber cargo was now adrift in the maelstrom of breaking seas, tumbling about like a thousand battering rams. It was into this swirling and heaving jumble of timbers that Captain Neale ordered the boats lowered but, significantly, refused to board one of them himself. Instead he sought refuge on the top of the pilothouse. When the *Myron* went down the rush of air from her forward spaces burst out the sides of the pilothouse, and Captain Neale, still on the roof, was catapulted into the water, with the flimsy boats carrying his crew. The *Adriatic* tried vainly to effect a rescue, but the thundering seas and the proximity of the exposed shoreline made it impossible. Another great ore ship hove on the scene and did what she could to get to the men in the boats, but, like the *Adriatic,* she could not get close enough. The men in the lifeboats were trying desperately to row out clear of the grinding sea of timbers, but the distance to the ore ships was too great. Rescue lines fell short or could not be grasped by freezing hands. Finally the little boats were swept into the fatal seas of timber and there was nothing to do about it.

The *Adriatic* duly reported the wreck at the Soo, and Coast Guard crews patrolled the shoreline of Whitefish Point for a week. They found lumber, enough to build a town. It was in jumbled masses and already partly covered by ice. There were many small, light pieces of wood that could or could not have been part of the lifeboats, but of the seventeen men who had left the *Myron* in them there was no trace. The writhing timbers had acted like a giant grinding machine, whose product Lake Superior had forever claimed.

Shipping men were still adding up the toll of that wildest of Novembers when word was flashed from Ft. William, Ontario, that Captain Neale was alive! An alert mate on an upbound freighter had spotted what seemed to be the top of a pilothouse, floating in the steamer lanes. When the ship drew closer they could make out the figure of a man on it.

They lowered a boat and soon tender hands lifted Captain
Neale to the deck and then to a warm cabin.

The Captain then related how an errant current or eddy
had somehow carried his pilothouse raft away from the crashing timbers and out into the lake. Numerous ships had
passed nearby, but the seas were still high and he had nothing
to signal with. He was numb with exposure and exhaustion
when the sharp-eyed mate spotted him.

But what about the *Miztec*, cast adrift to shift for herself?

Her anchors had dragged considerably, but when they
finally got a "bite" on foul bottom they held her resolutely.
She lost her deck load and there was enough lumber on the
beach to build still another town, but she held steady into
the face of the seas, surviving them as a good schooner hull
is supposed to do. When things had quieted down a bit a
freighter towed her to quiet waters in the lee of Whitefish
Point, where she waited patiently and in good grace for a
tug to fetch her in.

Some wreckage of ships that perish undoubtedly does
come ashore somewhere, but the shoreline of Lake Superior
today is as forbidding and lonely as it was centuries ago.
Years later, perhaps, a bit of something is found that brings
back memories of ships and men that are gone forever. But
unless found wreckage has some identifying features or
markings it means nothing and could have been washed up
on the beach a generation ago or only yesterday. Relatives of
lost sailors have spent an entire summer searching the
beaches and rocky coves of the south shore looking for clues.
There are instances of wooden hatch covers being found,
but most ships had wooden hatch covers and they look much
alike.

There are rare occasions of wreckage of a particular ship
being found and identified as such, and then it is almost always by accident. And when the fate of the vessel and her

people is already known it is relatively unimportant, except to lake historians and collectors of relics.

Take that day in August of 1920, nine months after the great November gales of 1919. When J. W. Le B Ross, superintending engineer of the Canadian locks at the Soo, confirmed the finding of the bodies of Magnus Peterson and two other crewmen of the *John Owen* on Parisian Island, he added, almost as an afterthought, in a letter to George A. Marr:

"I am also informed from another source that the stern portion of the steamer *Myron* lies on the shore near Coppermine Point."

No doubt the affairs of the *Myron's* people were as tangled as those of the crew of the *John Owen*. If so, John T. Kelley could express a hearty measure of sympathy for those responsible for settling them.

More than two years after his ship had gone down Mr. Kelley was still writing letters, signing affidavits and making numerous depositions. It was bad enough when letters to the next of kin of the ship's itinerant firemen and coal passers were returned marked "no such address." Worse yet were the letters seeking information on missing loved ones who might or might not have been on the *John Owen*.

Colonel Edward J. Parker of the Salvation Army's New York headquarters sought to locate a seventeen-year-old youth named Clarence Franklin Knight.

"We are given to understand that he was not on the *Myron*," wrote Colonel Parker. "His mother is very anxious to learn something concerning his death and we have been referred to you."

Mr. Kelley could find no such name on the crew list. But then again, Clarence Franklin Knight might have been any one of those who signed on at Duluth with whatever name seemed to fit the occasion.

Soon after the *John Owen* went down Mr. Kelley began receiving letters from one Andrew Nelson, a Duluth attorney who represented the estates of Magnus and Emma Peterson. Most of these requested affidavits and depositions relative to wages due and, for insurance claims, affirming legally that Magnus and Emma Peterson were indeed employed on the *John Owen* and did indeed perish as the ship went down with all hands. The matter was further complicated by the fact that neither of the Petersons was a United States citizen and both had surviving parents, in Norway and Sweden. This brought the consulates of both countries into the picture with more forms to be filled out and letters to be written.

As the months went on Andrew Nelson also became the legal representative of the estate of John L. Forschner, the *John Owen*'s first assistant engineer. It was the same old story of more letters, depositions, affidavits and insurance claim forms to be attested to. Most of these matters required Mr. Kelley to visit the office of Alexander C. Mackenzie, a Cleveland attorney who represented Andrew Nelson's office.

But finally Mr. Kelley had enough. Early in January of 1922 he wrote Nelson: "Now, brother Nelson, this is getting to be a continued story. If you need any more depositions have your attorney come to our office. . . ."

It is much better, as one can see, for the men in the shipping offices if their vessels complete their assigned voyages and deliver their cargoes without coming to grief. There are all manner of unpleasant details to be attended to, about all of which the average landlubber would know little and care less. For long after the headline of a wreck or missing ship has been forgotten, there are still those intimately concerned in her affairs and those of her people.

# 10

⚓

# The Curse of the Copper

The Chippewas were saying more than a hundred years ago that a fatal, inescapable curse or evil spirit went with the copper from the rich lodes of the Lake Superior country. It began, so their legend has it, with the prehistoric tribes that once mined the metal on bleak Isle Royale, far out in Lake Superior. These primitive peoples disappeared unaccountably and completely centuries ago, leaving only evidence of their digging and the ruins of crude smelters for present day geologists to ponder over.

The curse, some claimed, was responsible for the early and untimely death, in 1845, of Douglass Houghton, the man who at the age of thirty-four discovered the first copper deposits on the rugged Keweenaw Peninsula of upper Michigan. Houghton was drowned in a canoe accident before news of his discoveries brought hopeful hordes of prospectors and speculators storming northward to the cold and forbidding land of copper. He didn't live to see the booming Tamarack, Mowhawk and Calumet and Hecla mines or the new towns his explorations made possible—Hancock, Eagle

River, Houghton and Copper Harbor. Neither would he have dreamed that someday the Keweenaw Peninsula and its mining properties would be as well known in financial circles as Nome, Skagway and the Klondike were later to become. For eighty years the names and places of the Keweenaw area figured importantly in the world copper market. And in all fairness to Douglass Houghton, it probably wouldn't have made much difference. For he was an explorer and scientist, not a speculator, promotor or exploiter.

Although fortunes were made and lost in the copper lands of Michigan, from the tip of the peninsula all the way down to Ontonagon, they were made and lost by men who haunted the brokerage houses and who had never ventured within a thousand miles of the lonely land.

The curse, however, did indeed seem to cast a spell on many who wrested for the metal with their hands. An amazing number of those who came to seek wealth were city men who knew little about the incredibly cold and long northern winters or the cruel thaws of spring that turned the grim country into a bog. The imaginative souls who stuck it out prospered and became the pioneer families in the new towns that sprang up. A few, because there was no escape, sweated it out for a single winter, laboring in the shafts and counting the days until the first schooner of spring. Others left their bones to whiten in the summer sun of the Keweenaw country.

The curse or evil spirit, according to the Chippewas, followed the copper everywhere, even aboard the ships that bore it southward to the lower lake ports and the railroad lines. In any event, and it is recorded history, while many ships obviously arrived at their port of call safely, copper-laden ships, whether sail or steam, seemed to inherit a destiny of disaster, a malignant power that brought storm, death and destruction. It plagued not only those who took

the copper from the earth but those who carried it away and, generations later, the men who sought to retrieve the copper from the holds of the doomed vessels.

A case in point—and it is but one of many—is that of the ill-fated three-masted schooner *Kitty Reeves,* lying somewhere off Tawas Point, at the northern end of Saginaw Bay, in Lake Huron. On the evening of November 7, 1870, the *Kitty Reeves* was laboring in a heavy gale off the point, barely maintaining steerageway as white water sluiced her decks and a driving snow plastered her rigging and superstructure. Finally, in desperation, the anchor was dropped to keep the ship headed into the wind. The situation apparently grew progressively worse, for later the Captain and crew of eight launched the lifeboat and after a terrifying night in the open boat miraculously managed to beach their craft at Point Lookout, fifteen miles to the south. But during the wild night the ship's anchor chain snapped, and the *Kitty Reeves,* after drifting for several hours, was overwhelmed and sunk with her cargo of copper ingots, worth $250,000 on today's market.

For years, when the water was clear and the sun in the right position, the stub of a mast could be seen underwater, marking the schooner's grave. But roving ice fields during the winters eventually wiped away the only clue as to her location, and the *Kitty Reeves* was left to her fate and the shifting sands that finally covered her hull.

During the eighty years following her sinking, various people organized salvage expeditions to recover the valuable copper, but in every case bad weather, accidents to equipment or other unforeseen difficulties sent them home wiser and poorer. Then, in 1952, the month of August found two rival expeditions anchored a quarter mile apart and 2000 feet off the beach, each claiming to be hove-to over the wreck, lying under 20 feet of water and an estimated 12 feet of sand. One salvage crew, with the 60-foot schooner *Bercliff* as headquarters, was led by a Saginaw oil-lease broker, Wilford G. Shannon. A short distance away, aboard the *Gary B.,* activity was being directed by eighty-two-year-old Julius Roth, a tall, white-haired and bespectacled retired general storekeeper of Danbury, Ohio. But even while storekeeping Roth had long been a victim of "copper fever" and had spent ten years in research to find the hulk.

After a long hunt he found an old gentleman named Frank Black, who, as a boy, had lived near the lifesaving station at Tawas Point. From Black he learned just where the *Kitty Reeves* had been anchored. To determine in which direction she might have been driven after losing her anchor, he made contact with the U.S. Weather Bureau for the direction and velocity of the wind on the night of November 7, 1870. Strangely, the earliest official records for Lake Huron winds began on November 8, the day after the schooner went adrift! The wind on November 8, however, had been from the northeast. Roth figured out an approximate drift line and then worked with Dr. W. G. Keck, a Michigan State College geophysicist, who rigged up a pair of underwater metal detectors.

In 1947, as Keck and Roth were dragging the detectors along the lake bottom, Keck saw the needle of one instrument react strongly.

"We've found her," he shouted triumphantly to Roth.

But Roth was still a long way from the coveted copper. As strong currents off the point tore away one marker buoy after another, they were frequently compelled to relocate their prize. Roth finally bought an old sandsucker in Toledo to remove the sand covering the wreck, but the aged ship filled and sank at her moorings soon after arriving at Tawas.

The 1952 shenanigans off Tawas beach attracted national attention and interest. Sentiment was with Roth, who had done all the preliminary work and research only to have the Shannon group move in when the wreck was located.

But was it located? During the summer both sides issued countless statements. Shannon, the oil-lease broker, using a professional diver, once announced that his crew had drilled into wood, presumably the deck planking of the *Kitty Reeves*. Roth claimed that the planking couldn't be that of the copper ship because his own boat was anchored right on the target and that Shannon's boast was merely to discourage him into abandoning the site. Both groups admitted, however, that they would need sandsuckers and clam-shell power shovels to remove the sand.

Bad fall weather put a finish to salvage work for that year, and Roth, overtaken by ill health, was forced to call it quits for the time being. No more work was ever undertaken by the Shannon group either and, according to the records, the *Kitty Reeves* is still there, her cargo holds still to be broached. Every year, though, there are more stories about ambitious salvagers, most of them without the means or equipment, heading for Tawas Point and the wreck of the *Kitty Reeves*.

During the Roth–Shannon episode the question was posed as to how possession of the cargo was to be established. Under admiralty law the first crew to establish possession could claim it, but nobody on the salvage boats were certain how that could be done.

"I guess the first one to bring up a copper bar owns it," said the nearest official legal authority, Reginald Barnet, Iosco County prosecutor.

It was suggested too, that each of the salvage ships might have been anchored over a copper hulk, only one of them the *Kitty Reeves*. Records certainly indicated that enough of them had been lost without trace to bring this within the realm of possibility.

Enterprising salvagers who worked on the wreck of the steamer *W. H. Stevens* were more successful, perhaps because they were well south of Chippewa country. The *Stevens,* a large 212-foot steamer owned by the Union Transit Company of Buffalo, was bound from Duluth to Buffalo with a cargo of flax and copper ingots when she burned and sank about twenty-three miles off Clear Creek, Ontario, in Lake Erie, on September 8, 1902. Days after the disaster R. Parry Jones, representing the salvage branch of Lloyds of London, in view of the exposed location, predicted that the wreck might never be found or any of the copper recovered. A devil-may-care salvager proved him wrong only a few weeks later by lifting $50,000 worth of ingots. Two years later sixty additional tons were salvaged. During World War II, with copper at a premium, a Detroit businessman backed an expedition that brought up really big tonnage. Another thirty tons, covered with soggy flax, is still within the hull. Divers reported that the *Stevens* is sitting on an even keel in eleven fathoms of water with her decks burned off.

There are many other copper-laden hulks in Lake Huron and Lake Erie, but in many cases there were no survivors to give them even an approximate location. Those who lived through the great storms that sank their vessels reported almost unanimously that they had been driven helplessly for hours before howling gales. Visibility was poor and in most cases they could speak but vaguely of where the wrecks lay.

Whenever there is mention of treasure salvage or valuable cargoes in sunken hulls, particularly copper, conversation invariably turns to the old *Pewabic,* a hulk that has lain off Thunder Bay Island, in Lake Huron, for nearly a century. If ever a ship was touched with the copper curse of the Chippewas it is the *Pewabic.* No other single wreck has claimed so many lives in unsuccessful salvage operations or brought more trouble, hardship and grief. Bankruptcy has been the usual harvest of the would-be salvagers and yet, through the years, her cargo of copper has lured many treasure hunters, each scornful of the legend of the curse and each certain that he could do what had brought only tragedy to his predecessors.

The *Pewabic* was almost new, a big combination passenger and package freighter, typical of a great fleet of similar steam vessels that succeeded the sailing schooners and preceded the long bulk carriers that now ply the lakes. She was downbound in Lake Huron when a collision with her own sister ship, the *Meteor,* sent her plunging to the bottom. Some said the *Pewabic*'s wheelsman was temporarily blinded by the setting sun. Others claim the wheelsman of the *Meteor* misunderstood an oral order. The setting sun, a mistaken order, God-knows-what: the brutal fact remains that early in the evening of a beautiful August day in 1865, with visibility unlimited and all gear in perfect working order, the *Meteor* smashed squarely into the *Pewabic's* side with such force that the latter foundered before many of her passengers and crew knew exactly what had happened. The *Meteor*, badly damaged and leaking, lingered only long enough to snatch up the few survivors, including Captain George McKay, before steaming full speed to the nearest port, Alpena, for emergency repairs.

When she took her fatal dive, the *Pewabic* carried down with her nearly one hundred passengers, five hundred tons of pure copper and her purser's safe, said to hold over $50,000 in gold. A second safe was later rumored to have been aboard, but the *Pewabic's* owners would neither confirm nor deny this.

At any rate, the *Pewabic* had scarcely settled on the sandy bottom of Lake Huron before prospective salvagers prepared to probe for her. Stories of her copper and gold circulated freely in lake ports, some estimates of their value exaggerated far beyond the bounds of reason or probability. But, whenever sunken treasure is mentioned, few question the facts but immediately begin to dream of salvage and riches to be plucked from the bottom of the lakes.

By the spring of 1866, numerous prosperous-looking individuals were arriving in Alpena with big talk of men and equipment on the way north to bring up the *Pewabic* or her cargo. In almost every case the equipment failed to arrive, met with disaster en route or, when it did arrive, proved to be completely inadequate. Lying in 175 feet of water, the *Pewabic* could only be reached by experienced divers backed by men of salvage skill and heavy equipment such as work barges, supply boats, cranes, air pumps and tools. Few of the would-be salvagers could supply these necessities but came to the scene anyhow, hoping to rent or borrow a salvage ship and hire the divers.

Into the 1900's the *Pewabic* lay, her copper and gold untouched while countless comic opera salvagers befouled her rigging with drag lines, anchors and worthless gear. In fifty years ten divers lost their lives in futile efforts to enter the hulk, yet there were always others ready to try again in the same patched-up suits and battered helmets. During the winters, glib promotors toured the Midwest organizing new expeditions, backed by the hard cash of factory workers and merchants who knew nothing of the risks entailed but who were easily swayed by the irresistible lure and romance of sunken treasure and quick wealth.

In July of 1909 the first "big" expedition with full equipment and supplies came to Alpena with the announced intention of "getting the copper and safe before the summer is over." Heading the group, backed by a New York syndicate, was William Petry, inventor of an armored diving suit said to have been tested to a depth of 250 feet. Despite good intentions and a summer of hard work, the expedition called it quits early in October. Sudden storms had swept away their buoys, unexplained accidents delayed the divers and mechanical breakdowns rendered lifting equipment useless. Truly, as one of the backers said later, "The *Pewabic* is a hoodoo ship, she seems to cast an unnatural spell over all who try to salvage her gold and copper!"

Next came Dr. Fernando Staud of Chicago, who had plans to raise the entire ship with a system of canalons. The canalons, actually round tanks about the size and shape of oil-tank cars, were to be sunk beside the *Pewabic*. A net of chains was to be placed under the hull by divers and connected to the tanks. By pumping air into the tanks, Dr. Staud hoped to float the wreck. Apparently the good doctor wanted more than the copper and gold, for his purpose in floating the ship was to dismantle it, the planking to be made into canes, egg cups and other souvenirs and the ironwork to be sold for whatever it would bring as mementoes. Small bits of wreckage brought up by the draglines of previous searchers had sold at such a high price on the Lake Huron shore that Dr. Staud estimated the hulk to be worth as much as its elusive cargo. There was grisly logic here, for the doctor doubtless recalled tales of the burning of the steamer *Phoenix* in Lake Michigan in 1847 with the loss of over two hundred fifty Dutch immigrants. The wooden shoes of the victims, drifting ashore for weeks after the disaster, brought high prices all along Lake Michigan's easterly shore, so high, in fact, that an unscrupulous Chicagoan imported thousands of new ones that he peddled for years as genuine souvenirs of the *Phoenix* disaster!

After laboring for three months, during which Lake Huron produced her usual quota of bad weather and hard luck, the doctor threw up his hands and left the scene forever. For years the huge black tanks lay corroding on the shore, monuments to another expedition under the spell of the Chippewa curse.

In 1917 the Leavitt Deep Sea Diving Company came to Thunder Bay with tugs, sea buoys, work barges and a new type of diving gear. Again came the process of locating the wreck. For weeks the tugs swept the area until eventually, 17½ miles east-southeast of North Point Light, the drag rail stopped suddenly, straining the towing cables almost to the breaking point. Slowly the vessels were backed until they were directly over the obstruction. The railroad rail that had been trailing in the water was hoisted up for examination. On the rail were flakes of green paint—green paint from the *Pewabic's* superstructure! Quickly the wreck was buoyed off and one tug hastened to port for the diving barge.

Early the next morning, Oliver H. Shirley, chief diver for the Leavitt organization, was lowered over the side of the barge to examine the wreck. Down he went, deeper and deeper until at last he stood on the forward deck of a long vanished ship. Shirley had studied drawings of the *Pewabic* until he knew her every detail.

In less than five minutes he called excitedly over his headphone, "This is it, we've found the *Pewabic!*"

There have been many versions of Shirley's first trip through the ghostly passages within the hulk. He opened stateroom doors and found the skeletons of those trapped by the ship's incredibly swift plunge down. Clothing still hung from pegs in the wardroom. Opened trunks were lined up in orderly fashion and dishes were still in the pantry racks. Before giving the signal to pull him up, Shirley looked into the purser's cabin for the much talked about safe. He found no safe but instead a large hole in the floor. His guess was that the shock of the vessel hitting bottom caused the heavy safe to crash through the decking into the fo'c'sle. At any rate, the safe could wait. Shirley was eager to get back to the diving barge where anxious crews waited to hear of the wondrous sights below them.

Within a week permanent buoys had been set out, a barge with lifting equipment was anchored over the wreck and the serious business of getting the cargo began. At night, as the salvage crews rested ashore, they dined on sardines, pickles, salmon, preserves and other canned delicacies brought up from the *Pewabic's* galley and drank bottled beer that had been in the hulk for over fifty years.

It is estimated that the Leavitt group recovered about one hundred fifty tons of copper before the *Pewabic*, or perhaps it was the Chippewa, jinx popped up. A dispute arose over title to the recovered copper. Rumor had it that the United States Government claimed title to the copper that was daily being piled up on the dock at Alpena. This seems irregular, since the *Pewabic* had been down long enough to be within the public domain; but, bearing in mind that the United States had just become an active combatant in World War I and copper being a vital material, it is more likely that a "freeze" had been put on the price for which the metal could be sold. In any event, the Leavitt Deep Sea Diving Company called off further work and abandoned both the wreck and the salvaged copper.

Far more spectacular than the copper, however, were the souvenirs that diver Shirley brought up from the hulk, which even today are priceless relics owned by his daughter, Mrs. Gladys Roberts of Rossford, Ohio. Mrs. Roberts has plates from the galley with the crest of the *Pewabic*'s owners still visible, a silver goblet from the passenger's dining salon, box-toed shoes, stateroom keys, a padlock, a thimble and ornamental iron from the cabin doors. From the uniform coat of Captain McKay, which was found in the pilothouse, Shirley clipped the brass buttons that have since been made into cuff links.

The wrecks of the sunken copper ships are high on the list of worthwhile and salvageable cargoes littering the bottom of the Great Lakes. Even at the price of twenty-four cents a pound, a figure established by the International Materials Conference in 1951, a few hundred tons of copper adds up to a respectable sum. Scrap dealers were quoting fifty cents a pound in 1965. But locations are decidedly vague, and the wreck of a copper-laden ship looks the same as any of the hundreds of schooners, brigs or steamers on the bottom. Indeed, when the vanished treasure ships weren't carrying copper they were busy freighting lumber, salt, machinery, shingles, stone or any of a hundred other cargoes. The problem is one of exploration, detection and investigation . . .

eliminating the valueless hulks from those with really worth-while cargoes.

But the days of underwater exploration by hard-suit divers and their air lines, compressors, work boats, decompression chambers and other gear are gone. This is the day of the free-moving skin diver, and it is here in the searching phase where time and money are saved. A pair of experienced skin divers working from a small boat can examine, explore and measure a hull in a fraction of the time taken by the old-timers in their cumbersome suits and trailing lines. No need for tugs with pumps or compressors or crews to attend the divers or, for that matter, no need for work boats, barges or lifting equipment—until the right wreck is found! Relatively new, too, are the improved Fathometers, underwater sound scanners plotting the contour and profile of the bottom. And there are underwater radar and vastly improved metal detectors, all tools of the progressive salvager.

And with the coming of the age of the skin diver there is every probability that exploration and salvage on the Great Lakes will reach proportions never dreamed of a scant generation or two ago. Already skin divers have reported finding old wrecks in all the Great Lakes, and with the help of historians and researchers they may solve many a century-old mystery. Perhaps, too, if the Chippewa legend doesn't hold true, they'll find some of the old copper-laden vessels that other generations of divers and salvagers have dreamed about and longed for in vain.

# 11

⚓

# The Ship That Smoked from
# the Wrong End

From the low and verdant shoreline of Ontario, where on languid summer days the endless fields of corn and tobacco cast a green halo above Pigeon Bay, Point Pelee just sharply and ominously about ten miles south into Lake Erie. A single road parallels its coast. Its eastern exposure is largely inletted marsh land, a haven for thousands of migrating geese and ducks.

Southwest, from the very tip of the point, roughly nine miles as the crow flies, is Pelee Island, also in Canadian waters. It too is low, largely agricultural and is known for its fantastic population of pheasants. Between the point and the island is Pelee Passage, a narrow deep-water channel through which must pass all the deep draft vessels outbound from the Detroit River and Bar Point to the south shore Lake Erie ports and the north shore Port Colborne, Ontario, gateway to the Welland Canal and the St. Lawrence Seaway.

Well toward the Ohio shore is little-used South Passage,

of convenience primarily to vessels trading out of Sandusky, but offering a still more confining course and lesser depths for really large carriers.

Pelee Passage is, in a manner of speaking, sort of a Port Said of North America. Through the narrow channel passes a steady parade of the great bulk freighters that nurture the steel ports with iron ore and limestone. Others are deep down with coal, sulphur, salt, grain or pig iron. Sharing the channel more frequently now are the saltwater tramps of many flags and nations. Bringing the commercial harvests of Europe, South America, the Orient and the Middle East to our freshwater ports, they slog along outward bound with the exports from the mills and factories of the Midwest or full-bellied with wheat from our Plains states or Canada's great grain-growing provinces.

Unfortunately, Pelee Passage is flanked with a nightmare of foul water, not only in its confined approaches, but immediately adjacent to the channel itself. A scattered wilderness of rock reefs and nested boulders waits to snatch the bottom from any deep draft vessel that wanders from the charted course. With the exception of the dread shifting and sucking sands of Sable Island, off the coast of Nova Scotia, or the infamous Cape Hatteras, probably no single area has claimed more ships.

Beginning with Southeast Shoal Light, which marks the easterly approach, the bottom is foul and shoal to the north. A submerged rock and gravel spit extends over two miles out from the point itself, and East Shoal, with a least swept depth of only eleven feet, is another murderous trap. South of the deep-water channel, as an upbound ship nears Pelee Passage Light, lies Middle Ground Shoal, while immediately to the north is Grubb Reef, an assassin with a long list of victims.

The channel is marked with lighted buoys to segregate upbound and downbound traffic, and the adjacent shoals are also marked with a variety of navigational aids. Flashing white or red buoys and radar reflective spars mark the extent of the shoal waters.

As if the vicissitudes of the receding great glacier had not already created a veritable cul-de-sac of hazards for Great Lakes mariners, the geographical peculiarities add another. Cold fronts, moving off the Ontario shore, meet the warmer water of Lake Erie, often producing dense and lingering fogs. "Muzzlers," the lakes sailors call them. Pelee Passage in any weather is not to be taken lightly. In fog it is extremely perilous.

Generations of early settlers and fishermen reaped bountiful harvests of wagon wheels, trunks, lumber, shingles and furniture from the shores after schooners and immigrant steamers left their bones on the reefs or collided in the enveloping fogs.

Little wonder then that those responsible for the safety of shipping require saltwater tramp ships, accustomed to plenty of water under their keels, to take aboard a Great Lakes pilot. Pelee is but one of the unfamiliar hazards they face, but it is one of the most formidable. Sailors refer to the whole Pelee Passage and Southeast Shoal area as the "middlegrounds." And masters of foreign tramps, when it is possible, much prefer to transit the middlegrounds in daylight, pilot or no.

The plates and ribs of many ships, and some with hulls still intact, are strewn over the middlegrounds bottom. A few have cargoes that salvagers have sought for years. Six wrecks, only a fraction of the total, but adjacent to the steamer tracks and possible hazards in heavy weather, are marked on the Lake Erie charts and dutifully noted in the U.S. Lake Survey's "Great Lakes Pilot." They show, for example, that the wreck of the steamer *Charles B. Packard* has a depth of water over it of only 21 feet. And near it, unidentified, lies another hulk with the same clearance. The wreck of the schooner *Armenia* lies near the vessel course a little over three miles NW by W from Pelee Passage Light. Still another wreck, the steamer *Specular,* lies the same distance SE, ½E from the light with a swept depth of 17 feet over it. Nearby are the remains of the barge *Tasmania* and the steamer *Jay Gould.*

For a hundred years, before gyroscopic compasses, automatic direction finders and radar minimized the incidence of human error, Pelee Passage became, in its own insidious and peculiar way, the graveyard of the Great Lakes. Marine and news columns of the mainland cities had occasion to make frequent mention of sinkings, collisions, fires and strandings in or around it. Somewhat like a funnel through which the majority of deep draft vessels had to pass, it was inevitable that some should come to grief.

One of the most bizarre disasters, involving shipwreck and fire, was one that Joseph Boyer should have been involved in. He wasn't, simply because he missed a streetcar.

Boyer was an oiler on the wooden steamer *George Stone,* which, on an October morning in 1909, was moored at a Detroit dock, taking on stores while her chief engineer was attending to some minor repairs. The *Stone* was downbound after delivering a cargo of coal to Port Huron. With the assurance that it would be another hour before the ship would get under way, Boyer, a Detroit resident, requested time to dash home for some cold weather gear.

Captain Paul Howell nodded assent.

But these were tempestuous days along the waterfront. The first of the seamen's unions was making a strong bid for recognition, and a strike was even then in progress. Organized mariners and their sympathizers lurked at every dock to discourage, physically, if necessary, the signing on of non-union men or the sailing of ships manned by them. The shipping companies were resisting bitterly. Fights and scuffles were frequent.

Just such a situation was shaping up as the *Stone* was being provisioned and readied for another voyage. A knot of strikers gathered, and in short order insults were being exchanged. The union men were being particularly obnoxious and personal in their remarks. Captain Howell, sensing that a brawl was imminent, suddenly decided that he could do without an oiler.

"Give me steam, mister," he bellowed down the voice pipe to the engine room.

Then, stepping out on the bridge wing, he signaled for the lines to be cast. Ringing "full astern," he grabbed the wheel himself and backed his vessel into the channel.

Meanwhile Boyer, having missed a streetcar, arrived on the scene as the disgruntled unionists were pelting the fleeing *Stone* with rocks. The men on the ship replied with chunks of coal that chanced to be convenient.

Wisely, the tardy oiler ducked into a shanty, where the only other occupant, the elderly dock watchman, had enjoyed a good view of the fracas with complete immunity.

"Golly, son, you sure missed a jim-dandy of a scrap," cackled the dock guardian.

At Ashtabula, where a high wire fence and dock police kept possible troublemakers far from the big coal dumpers, the *Stone* took on a cargo of 2800 tons of soft coal consigned to Racine, Wisconsin. It was a familiar burden, and the *Stone* accepted it without undue strain although it was piled up level with her hatch combings. By the time the last carload rumbled down the chute she had assumed her customary "squat" or loaded stance.

At 10 A.M. on Monday morning, having observed and entered into the log that the wind was moderate and holding steady from the northwest, Captain Howell pulled twice on the whistle cord, saw the hawsers come snaking in, and swung the engine order telegraph indicator to "full ahead." Clearing the Ashtabula breakwater, the *Stone* steamed three miles due north into Lake Erie before he ordered her hauled to port on the course for Southeast Shoal Light. Then, after witnessing his vessel swinging around to her proper bearing, he turned the helm over to the first mate and went below to get some sleep.

By all accepted standards the *Stone* was a sturdy, well-found vessel, or as sturdy and seaworthy as any of the weary wooden steamers still earning their keep despite the growing trend to larger ships built of steel. But she was deeply laden, had hidden ills and was quite unprepared for what lay in store for her. While the wind held from the northwest she nosed into the modest swells, developing an easy pitch and lazy roll. Two hours after leaving port the first mate noted in the log that the wind had, quite suddenly, backed into the east and showed every sign of becoming a bit of a snorter.

By late afternoon the following seas had acquired considerable stature, climbing over the after rail with monotonous regularity. The pitching motion was severe now, and the *Stone*'s timbers and frames began a whining, creaking lament that could be heard above the rush of wind and water. At best she could boast of a plodding six-knot pace and the great, white-topped seas that mounted their attack from astern found her an easy, slow-moving target.

Captain Howell, long since aroused from his sleep, pondered the problems the reversal of wind direction had brought down upon him. He could, as the first mate tentatively suggested, turn to port in an attempt to run for shelter behind the Fairport Harbor or Cleveland breakwaters. But the Captain was aware of his vessel's infirmities. Turning would necessarily put the *Stone* in the trough of the seas, and she would be taking them green over her decks all the way. This, he concluded, unhappily, she was not prepared to do.

"No, mister," he said to the mate, "I'm afraid we're going to have to keep 'er steady as she goes."

Moments later, from below, came word that some of the planking was beginning to work, admitting a modest accumulation of water. But it was nothing, the Captain was assured, that the ship's pumps could not handle, as they did, indeed, quite handily.

Through Monday night and all day Tuesday Captain Howell nursed his ship onward toward Pelee Passage. The planking, now under assault for thirty-six hours, was working out long gouts of caulking. Jets now spurted in with each vindictive sea where trickles had shown before. The pumps were going full power and scarcely holding their own against the quickening inrush!

At midnight Tuesday the *Stone* was well into the middle-grounds when the second engineer burst into the pilothouse.

"The pumps keep stopping, sir! The chief says they keep clogging with coal dust and we can't clean them fast enough!"

There was water in the cargo hold now, too, plenty of it judging from the way the *Stone* answered her helm. Blessed with adequate power for her size, she was, under normal circumstances, quite lively. Now she responded slowly and had developed an ominous tendency to fall off into the troughs. What's more, she no longer wanted to follow her course. She kept sheering off to starboard, where the worst of Point Pelee's dread shoals awaited. Visibility was poor, and since passing Southeast Shoal Light the Captain had not sighted a single buoy that would give any indication of his exact position.

Faced with a situation he could scarcely hope to cope with successfully, Captain Howell made his decision. He grabbed second mate John Hindle by the shoulders and shouted, "Drop both anchors—we may sink, but I'm damned if we're going ashore here."

The anchors went thundering down, their chains writhing in a shower of sparks.

"Give me about six hundred feet of chain," he roared. "This is foul bottom, and they may not grab right away."

This proved to be an understatement of grand proportions. The anchors not only failed to hold, they barely slowed the progress of the *Stone,* being driven onward by those towering graybeards that came roaring in from astern. The water in the engine room had risen to the boiler grates now, and the sweating firemen could not muster enough steam to hold her, even though they had her engine thrashing full astern!

At 2:30 in the morning, still dragging both her anchors, the *Stone* went hard on Grubb Reef! She slid on with considerable momentum and ground half her length over a seemingly endless nest of boulders. Once there in her unyielding bed she seemed to sigh resignedly, like a long-abused dray horse that has somehow found her way back to her stall, there to collapse, awaiting whatever fate life still held in store for her.

Driven forward by seas that stampeded over the fantail to flood their quarters shoulder high with icy water, the aft crew clawed their way along the deck rails to join the Captain, mates and forward crew in the pilothouse. All that night they could feel their ship twisting uneasily as the weight of the falling seas thundered over the deck and hatches while the rising ones assaulting her stern sought to drive her farther onto the reef.

Daylight came after what seemed an eternity. And Grubb Reef, in daylight, was no happier sight than it had been in darkness. All about them the seas boiled and seethed around a vast wasteland of submerged boulders, showing themselves briefly in the trough of the seas, like bashful porpoises.

At the Captain's direction the crewmen took turns climbing the foremast, waving a bed sheet at distant vessels laboring through Pelee Passage. Strangely, although at least a dozen passed, either upbound or downbound, not one saw the sheet being waved so frantically and hopefully by the *Stone*'s discouraged men. They shouted hoarsely and futilely. A fireman knelt in the pilothouse and cried unashamedly.

"They must be blind," raged Mate Hindle. "Any sailor would know from our position that we're in trouble."

But now, even though they were as sore beset as sailors can be, another calamity befell them. During the excitement, as they were trying to attract attention, the oil lamp inside the pilothouse was upset, and in seconds the structure was ablaze! Driven from their only haven, they could do little but cling to the rails and pray. Blistered one moment from the intense heat, they were doused the next by the seas that came romping the length of the deck.

The fire was raging through the bow now, and as the black smoke from the oil, rags and paint in the dunnage room began to tower into the sky it brought new hope, at least to wheelsman John Connors.

"They didn't see our sheet," he shouted, "but at least they can see the smoke."

Captain Howell offered little hope. "Smoke is exactly what they expect to see from a steamer," he said dryly.

Up to this point the Captain had refused to consider launching the boats. The *Stone*'s position on a rocky reef, in his opinion, rendered unlikely a successful abandonment of the ship. First, the seas were still so high that it would be in the order of a miracle if they were not smashed immediately against the ship. Secondly, the entire area between the stranded ship and the nearest land, Point Pelee, was

being churned into a maelstrom of white water and glistening rocks that would soon wreck a small boat.

He had held to his conviction even though most of the
crew indicated a willingness to take their chances. But now,
really, there was no choice. With the bow of their ship ablaze
and exploding paint cans arching up from the dunnage
room like skyrockets, the crewmen followed their captain aft.
With each mounting sea they grasped the rails until it had
hissed on, and while its angry spume still lashed at their
legs they edged another step or two toward their goal. Finally
they climbed the pipe ladder to the roof of the after cabins.
With all but the bow besieged by water there was little
likelihood that fire would consume the entire ship. But
there was every possibility that what was left would soon be
reduced to matchwood.

Having taken the ship, Lake Erie now sought her people.
Indeed, although he made no mention of what was on his
mind, Captain Howell, feeling the stern lift and pound,
wondered what had held the *Stone* together this long. Spray
was flying over her stack, and the entire after end shook and
quivered as the full weight of tons of water dropped rhyth-
mically over her stern counter.

"We'll lower the wooden boat on the port side first," said
the Captain. "If it stays afloat some of us will get in and try
to reach the lighthouse and get help."

The boat was almost instantly swept under the *Stone's*
stern, where the first big sea smashed it into a hundred
pieces, some of them coming aboard the ship with the sea.

"Now then, we'll try the steel boat on the starboard side,"
said Captain Howell, trying to keep from showing the tension
he felt.

But strangely, the urge to abandon the ship was no longer
unanimous. The men showed little enthusiasm as their cap-

tain and second mate Hindle unlashed the ropes of the falls
and began to let the boat down.

"Hop to it if you're going along," yelled Hindle.

A few clambered in. Altogether, when the boat dropped
into the valley between two seas, there were five seamen,
Captain Howell, Hindle and wheelsman Connors. The rest,
ten in all, retreated to what little shelter the smokestack,
ventilators and skylight afforded.

Miraculously, the lifeboat survived the first few big seas
while the men were shipping the oars and Captain Howell
was working the tiller into its sockets. Rowing like madmen
they pulled for Point Pelee. Seemingly the fates had relented
in their efforts to wipe out the *Stone's* people, for the seas
lifted the boat over the most formidable of the rocks. They
were almost in the clear when the men on the ship saw a
monstrous, snarling comber turn the lifeboat completely
over. In the seething surf breaking over the reef and the
smoke from the burning bow they failed to see any survivors.
As a matter of fact there were two, wheelsman Connors and
mate Hindle. Captain Howell and the five seamen were gone
forever!

At long last, from their battered refuge, those still aboard
the *Stone* saw two men stagger from the surf and collapse
on the beach. They were too far away to identify, but at
least someone would learn of the wreck and of those who
still awaited rescue.

So intent were they on the death drama in the shoals, even
though they themselves were faced with only a dim hope of
rescue before the ship broke up, that they failed to see a
steamer cautiously approaching. Its sonorous whistle startled
them almost out of their wits.

It was the *F. M. Osborn,* whose captain, Fred Dupuy, had
decided to investigate the strange sight of a steamer belching
smoke from the wrong end.

Captain Dupuy noted the missing boats, deduced that they had both been smashed and concluded that his own would likely be swept into the relentless combers that danced gleefully over Grubb Reef. The *Osborn* was a larger and more powerful steamer than the *Stone*. Even so, the seamanship Captain Dupuy displayed that day was the talk of the lakes for years.

The *Stone*, the Captain could see, was far up on the shoal, her bottom probably torn out and open to the seas. The only thing holding her together was the weight of her coal cargo, and even now this was beginning to surge out as the battering opened her planked hull. From the character of the seas that swirled and pounded at her stern he judged that the after third of the ship projected out over fairly deep water. He would have to take the *Osborn* right up to the *Stone*'s fantail if he were to save her people!

"Drop both anchors," he called down the voice pipe to the windlass room, even as Captain Howell had passed a similar order only twelve hours earlier.

But the *Osborn* had plenty of power, and with both big anchors dragging and the telegraph at "slow astern," Captain Dupuy maneuvered his ship closer and closer to the *Stone*'s fantail. On the bow of the *Osborn* her first mate motioned to the men on the *Stone* to get ready to jump.

Taking the wheel himself, with the second mate standing by the telegraph, Dupuy eased the *Osborn* in. The seas that punished the stranded ship were now assaulting the rescuers of her crew. Still, the big bow of the *Osborn*, though pitching fearfully, was slowly but steadily narrowing the gap. Her crew fully expected to feel their ship's bottom strike at any second!

At last Captain Dupuy planted his bow stem within five feet of the *Stone*'s fantail, and one by one, like puppets at command, the half-frozen men began jumping from the cabin roof to the hard steel fo'c'sle deck of the *Osborn*.

"Ten of us, that's it," called the rescued first engineer, "and thanks to God to ye, sir!"

While the survivors were being hustled below to the warmth of the boiler room and steaming mugs of coffee, Captain Dupuy rang up "full astern." Slowly, ever so slowly, her propeller churning desperately, the *Osborn* clawed her way free of Grubb Reef, hoisted her anchors and resumed her course to Detroit.

About the time the *Osborn* was completing her mercy mission, Captain Grubb, the light keeper at Point Pelee and the man for whose antecedents the reef was named, found Connors and Hindle on the beach, both still weak and exhausted. He helped them to the lighthouse, built a fire, made coffee and rounded up blankets before rushing off to report the wreck to the authorities. His shipwrecked guests were still sleeping the next morning when he climbed the tower to put out the oil light.

Shipwreck survivors, by all the laws of humanity and compassion, are traditionally welcomed home with tearful embraces, a hearty shaking of hands and all the spontaneous expressions of relief and joy the occasion demands. Alas, 'twas not so with the men of the *Stone*. News of the wreck and rescue traveled fast once Captain Grubb had flashed the word, and when the *Osborn* dropped them off at the same dock they had left only days before they were met by a welcoming committee of union men. Taunts led to curses and curses to blows. In seconds the dock was a madhouse of brawlers. Several times combatants rolled off into the river. Calmly, harbormaster William Ellison, who happened to be passing in his launch, fished them out with his pike pole.

The donnybrook was still in full swing when the police arrived. There was the dull thwacking sound of nightsticks making contact with solid pates, a shrilling of whistles, and in moments the fight was over.

Joseph Boyer had wanted to welcome his shipmates home, too, but once more he missed his streetcar, arriving just as the police were separating the warriors.

Again he sought the shelter of the watchman's shanty, and when that delighted but inactive witness saw him for the second time in a week he sighed sympathetically.

"Son, you just missed another jim-dandy of a scrap."

# 12

⚓

# Ah, Dear Sister

One of the first nuggets of knowledge acquired by a young student is the fact that the shortest distance between any two given points is a straight line.

And since, in the shipping business, the shortest distance is always the most economical, vessel owners, who must be concerned with fuel consumption, wages, provisioning costs and docking schedules, always have embarrassing questions to ask when a master, through course alterations, follows a devious route to his assigned port of call.

Always then, by time-tested tradition, the marine charts of the Great Lakes show prescribed courses and compass bearings to and from the various ports. Today they are largely the courses recommended by the Lake Carriers' Association, an industry group representing the major ship operators on the Great Lakes. Over the years, especially in the areas where the shipping lanes narrow, there has developed a system of specific upbound and downbound courses, designed to minimize the possibility of collision and to facilitate the movement of ship traffic through connecting straits and waterways, even in foul weather. In every instance, allowing for mandatory alterations to avoid headlands, land masses and shoal water, they are the shortest routes possible for laden vessels drawing not more than twenty-seven feet of water.

These standard course procedures are the result of long and sometimes tragic experience in an era when lake traffic was largely unregulated. The trials and tragedies of early shipmasters were costly in life and bottoms, but gradually, first by word of mouth between shipmasters and later by complete cooperation between masters, owners and managers, the following of certain specific courses became accepted practice. Steadily, too, came the results of surveys by the responsible governmental agencies. Hydrographic studies helped to mark and chart rocks and shoal waters. Soundings determined the safest channels and, where feasible and practical, there came expensive projects to remove dangerous obstacles, deepen heavily traveled channels and adequately buoy the hazards that remained. All of this became infinitely more practical and advantageous as steam replaced sail and the maintaining of a prescribed course became possible despite the vagaries of prevailing winds.

But long before the turn of the century, and even well into the 1900's, mariners passing through the Soo and bound for the neighboring Canadian ports of Fort William and Port Arthur, at the far northern end of Lake Superior, followed a standard course based largely on their own experience.

It was a relatively busy route. For years the ports were the center of activity for the northern railroad builders. Their rails, iron goods, hardware and machinery all came by ship. More recently, as the great grain-growing Canadian plains began yielding their astronomical harvests, the railroads they helped build have made Fort William and Port Arthur great grain shipping ports, the high elevators forming unmistakable profiles now familiar to generations of lake sailors.

The first prescribed course for the mariner bound the length of Lake Superior, with his port of call one of the twin ports, was relatively simple. Upbound, the cautious master leaving the shelter of the upper St. Marys River and approaching Whitefish Bay kept Gros Cap and Point Iroquois lights about equidistant, starboard and port. Then with Parisienne Isle well to starboard he next looked for Whitefish Point Light, off to port and his last mainland bearing for some time. Off to starboard he gave Outer Pancake Shoal a wide berth, steering roughly 310 degrees until safely past Caribou Island. Then he usually altered course to 320 to bring him on the Ft. William–Port Arthur track well to the north of dread Isle Royale, which flanks Thunder Bay and the entrance to the twin ports. The rocks and shoals off Isle Royale are sprinkled with the timbers and plates of many stout ships. These were not waters to be navigated in fog, and the prudent shipmaster, when his log, calculations or instinct told him Isle Royale was near, dropped his hooks and waited for clearing weather.

The course was clearly defined on the early charts, but with the rocks off Isle Royale always beckoning, the deepest water in Lake Superior under his keel and plenty of sea room to the north, who could fault a skipper for easing her off a few points to starboard to lessen the buffeting of a nor'west gale?

In any event, even though they deviated somewhat from the straight-course principle, early mariners were confident that their courses were over the deepest of the lake's waters, with known depths ranging from 600 to 1300 feet. Nevertheless, the entrance to Thunder Bay, with Pie Island to his port and Thunder Cape light safely on his starboard, was a welcome sight to any skipper.

Unaccountably though, a considerable number of sturdy vessels managed to disappear completely somewhere between the Soo and the twin ports. Since uncharted rocks, derelicts or shoal water could apparently be ruled out, it was assumed that the missing ships had suffered boiler explosions, over-powering seas or catastrophic structural failures. It had to be assumption, for none of the ships left any wreckage over which the experts could ponder. If they had left tragic mementoes, they would have been washed ashore along the hundreds of miles of rocky inlets, as bleak and unfriendly today as they were a century ago.

Storms probably account for the disappearance of the *Merchant,* in 1847, and the *W. W. Arnold* in 1869, both big schooners. But the *Manistee,* lost in 1883, was a passenger and freight steamer. Normally she would have been on the south shore route from Duluth, but after seeking shelter at Bayfield and waiting four days for better weather she hove anchor and departed. Another storm developed and she was seen no more. It is conceivable that her master, aware that miles of deep and open water lay to the north, turned his vessel into the face of the seas, hoping to ease her laboring until the gale blew itself out. In the case of the *Manistee* some wreckage came ashore days after she went down. And there were many others, steamers and schooners. How about the *Kamloops, Magellan, Bannockburn, Atlanta, Superior* and the *Pearl B. Campbell,* all of which vanished between 1856 and 1927? Or, for that matter, what happened to the big steel freighter *Benjamin Noble,* lost with all hands in 1914, only five years after she left her builder's ways?

Early records list many vessels "gone missing" on Lake Superior. Many were fine new craft, well turned out and manned by experienced crews. But such was often the lot of ships and sailors on Lake Superior where the disappearance of a ship was accepted philosophically as one of the inevitable hazards to be encountered by those who would wrest their living from Great Lakes commerce.

The Soo and much of the south shore of Lake Superior west of the St. Marys was Chippewa country. Voyageurs and fur trappers, sitting around the Chippewa camp fires heard strange tales and legends, most of them associated with their gods and demigods.

They heard much of Gitchee Manito, the good spirit; Matchi Manito, the evil spirit; the mighty Menaboju and the other chief spirits represented by the East, West, North and South Winds. But mostly they heard about Nanabazhoo, the cunning but kindly buffoon whose droll tales were likely to keep generations of Chippewas in high good humor. It was Nanabazhoo, legend has it, who brought fire to the Chippewas by turning himself into a hare, setting his fur ablaze at a neghboring tribe's camp fire and running home to his people. It was Nanabazhoo who once kicked a loon so hard in the rear that ever after all loons had a flat back with legs far aft. And it was Nanabazhoo who was swallowed, canoe and all, by a giant sturgeon, a fish so large, he related, that it might hold an entire Chippewa village in its mouth. Thereafter, when braves ventured out into Lake Superior to fish and failed to return, the Chippewas never blamed the elements but rather Nanabazhoo's fantastic sturgeon. Only the luckless braves were not as clever as Nanabazhoo, who escaped and lived to tell about it.

For generations the legend of the sturgeon was part of Chippewa mythology, and the yarns of his greatness grew with the years. Even in the early days of this century the Chippewas put some store in the giant sturgeon story, and occasionally the caprices of nature gave it stature and seemingly an element of truth.

Whenever a ship disappeared the white men set about hunting wreckage or clues to determine the cause. They never found an item of any significance, but the red men seemingly had the answer. It was just as Nanabazhoo had recounted—in the center of the lake lived a sturgeon so large that it would dwarf the white man's ships, demolishing them with a single flick of its tail if, indeed, he did not choose to swallow the entire vessel.

Every Chippewa who had ventured far out into the lake on fishing expeditions could relate that he had seen some evidence of the sturgeon; how suddenly, in the midst of a dead calm, a portion of the sea would quickly spawn a confused and seething maelstrom. Giant waves would develop from nowhere to rush at each other from opposite directions, exploding upon each other only to subside in a vortex of swirling white water. It was the great sturgeon, they knew, indulging in play and exercise near the surface.

How else could the mariner, even if he discounted the wild myths of the Chippewas, explain the curious incident of the Algoma Central Railway's steamer *Leafield?* During the summer of 1913 the *Leafield,* laden with railroad rails, was steaming under cloudless skies and on a flat calm sea at about the geographic center of Lake Superior. Without warning and with no indication of wind, the waters began to seethe

and heave. Great seas from opposing directions poured over
her from starboard and port. Plates and frames straining under the weight of the water that swept over her, the *Leafield*
was seemingly in the very center of a cyclonic gale except
that the sun was shining, the skies above were a clear blue
and there was no wind.

Shortly, however, the ship was once again in calm water,
and except for twisted railings and battered deck gear there
was no evidence that the vessel had been in violent water.

When the tale had made its way back to the Soo, the white
men explained it away as the shifting of underwater out-
croppings, the result of an earthquake reported in many
parts of the world at identical times. But in a Chippewa encampment hard by Point Iroquois, a wizened chief shook his
head knowingly. "It is even as Nanabazhoo has told our
fathers. It is there, in the center of the lake, that the giant
sturgeon plays on a warm summer afternoon."

Weeks later, when summer had turned into fall and winter
was ready in the wings waiting to make its presence known,
the steamer *James E. Davidson,* downbound in the same
area, was the leading character in still another strange episode. While proceeding through a heavy snowstorm the
*Davidson* was suddenly confronted by a single tremendous
sea. It thundered aboard directly over the bow, jarring the
ship to its very stern frame. In the firehold men were sent
tumbling, dishes cascaded from the galley racks and the captain was catapulted from his bunk. The anchor windlass
was torn from its bedplates and its controls smashed. Both
anchors dropped from their pockets while tons of chain
writhed madly about in the chain locker, tearing out the
hawsepipes and loosening bow plates. Far down by the head
and making water steadily, the *Davidson* just made the Soo
locks, almost in a sinking condition. When drydocked for

survey the inspectors found a great dent, ten feet long, in the ship's bottom.

Was this then the result of a collision with Nanabazhoo's great sturgeon? The marine surveyors who marked dozens of loosened rivets for replacement and the shipyard workers who made new plates and straightened her frames were sure it was a collision—but with something far more substantial than a sturgeon, however large.

Next on the mystery scene, sadly, perhaps prophetically, came a trio of identical vessels, unusual types to be found on the lakes, to say the least. They were born in the tumult of the Canadian Car and Foundry Plant's shipyard at Ft. William in 1918, three of the twelve minesweepers built there for the French government, to its designs. They came smoking down the ways ready for come what may: the *Navarin, Mantoue, Saint Georges, Leoben, Palestro, Lutzen, Seneff, Sebastapol, Malakoff, Bautzen, Inkerman* and *Cerisolles.* Their 145-foot hulls were very strongly braced and of heavier steel than is normally used in vessels of their size. Built for the heavy seas and rugged duty they would encounter in clearing the mines from stormswept saltwater reaches, they had beams of 22 feet and drafts of 13 feet. Coal-fired boilers drove 600 horsepower, triple-expansion, American-built engines.

Although hostilities had ceased just after the first nine were delivered and as the last three were completing their sea trials, the French, anticipating a long period, perhaps years, of locating and removing the thousands of coastwise mines planted during the war, still wanted two of the vessels. The third, since all were financed by the United States, was ordered to New York.

With uncertain futures ahead of them the trio, the *Inkerman,* the *Cerisolles* and the *Bautzen,* left Ft. William together. The *Inkerman* and *Cerisolles,* with French crews aboard, were ordered to part company with the *Bautzen* in the Bay of St. Lawrence and steam directly to France. All three left Ft. William under threatening skies the morning of November 24, 1918.

The full gale they encountered shortly after noon had been building up for some time. A storm cell born in the Northwest Territories gathered strength over the plains of Manitoba and Saskatchewan to hit Lake Superior with all its fury. On a broad front, from the Knife River in Minnesota to Jackfish Bay on the lonely northern shore, it swept the length and breadth of the lake. Along the south shore wind-driven streamers of black smoke told of long ships desperately seeking shelter behind Keweenaw Point, the Apostle Islands or the protective arm of Whitefish Point.

All that afternoon the gale continued to roar over the Sleeping Giant on Thunder Cape, whistling unhindered over Isle Royale and onward to the Soo. The *Bautzen,* her master apparently wanting plenty of sea room, kept a mile or two to the south of the course taken by the *Inkerman* and *Cerisolles.* During the day, with visibility poor and white water breaking over the *Bautzen*'s decks and cascading over her superstructure, only an occasional glimpse of the laboring vessels in the distance was possible.

That night the fathers, grandfathers and great-grandfathers of Lake Superior's mightiest graybeards were marching down the lake, thundering on like demented Crusaders determined to sweep and smash all before them. The puckish Nanabazhoo must have been battened down snugly in his tepee that night while the Chippewa's evil spirit, Matchi Manito, raged and ranted, whipping the lake into a blind, insane fury. The crests of the assaulting seas were dusted off in the form of flying spume as the minesweepers alternately rose to their very peaks and plunged into the dark and lonely valleys. Wrenched and rudely boarded by every sea, they suffered every indignity freshwater could inflict on them. The pitching and rolling placed a maximum of strain on the rudders and tailshafts. The engines quivered in their bedplates, and had they been lesser ships their topsides would have been torn away like orange crates. It was as if the elements had all combined to show once and for all that the finest, sturdiest examples of the shipwright's art could be torn asunder at their will.

On the second morning, even though the weather had moderated, the crewmen of the *Bautzen* could not find her sister ships on the heaving horizon. Assuming that they or perhaps even he had been driven off course by the gale, the *Bautzen's* skipper continued on to the locks at the Soo.

"Have the *Inkerman* and *Cerisolles* locked through?" he called to the lock tender who took the *Bautzen's* mooring cable.

"No, Captain, we've seen nothing of them here," was the reply.

Nor did the *Inkerman* and *Cerisolles* ever lock through. They had simply vanished from the face of the sea—two fine new ships and seventy-eight men.

Tugs and government search vessels scoured the lake without finding a trace of wreckage. Usually vessels broken and overwhelmed by storm leave a welter of debris—timbers, bunk frames, smashed lifeboats, cabin paneling, tables, chairs and a host of items that will float indefinitely. But the *Inkerman* and *Cerisolles* departed this earth leaving nothing.

The *Bautzen,* after lingering hopefully for a few days, locked through the Soo before the freezeup to make her sad journey to New York, leaving behind her another Lake Superior enigma.

But the war was over and Uncle Sam had no use for minesweepers, however new and fine. Eventually, as the fortunes of war go, she was sold to a Mr. Morrill Goddard, of New York, with the stipulation that she could not be used for commercial purposes. Goddard, delighted at the size and sea qualities of the vessel, converted it into a yacht, adding commodious cabins in the area originally intended for storage of recovered mines. Thus the *Bautzen,* altered and repainted, became the steam yacht *Rowena.*

And what a yacht she must have made. Graced with the lines of a merchant vessel rather than the sleek profile one associates with the sea-going gentry, the *Rowena* must nevertheless have been a comfortable, if expensive, craft to maintain. She required a considerable crew, several just to fire her boilers and operate her steam plant. And one wonders if her smoke, soot and cinders were welcome in the anchorages wherein lay the sleek but fragile greyhounds of the traditional yachting fleet?

But the frivolities of the yachting circle and safe moorings at Newport, New Bedford and Edgartown were not to be the lot of the *Rowena* for long.

In 1925, when the MacMillan Arctic Expedition was being organized, Commander E. F. McDonald, Jr., of Chicago, remembering the sturdy hull prescribed for the minesweepers, looked up the *Rowena,* née *Bautzen,* and bought her. Renamed the *Peary* in honor of the famed early polar explorer, the ship was outfitted and soon joined the auxiliary schooner *Bowdoin,* commanded by Donald B. MacMillan. Before departing for Etah, Greenland, the proposed base of the expedition, steel plates were welded over the portholes of the *Peary* to resist the ice pressures in infamous Melville Bay.

In a cabin off the *Peary's* shelter deck, young Commander Richard E. Byrd made his plans for what was to be the first polar exploration by air. Aft on the *Peary's* fantail were lashed three U.S. Navy amphibious planes that were later to be assembled for takeoff.

It had been Byrd's hope to chart and photograph a full

one million square miles of hitherto unexplored Arctic sea and land. But the expedition, under the auspices of the National Geographic Society, with the U.S. Navy cooperating, was plagued with ill luck. The winter had been unusually severe in the Arctic and the base anchorage at Etah, from where the planes were to take off on an extensive series of flights, was that year studded with roving icebergs and growlers, although the harbor was normally ice-free in the summer.

Almost continuous fog and frequent snowstorms vastly curtailed the airborne phase of the expedition, although other objectives were attained. The deck-bound scientists aboard both ships made extensive collections of marine life and the flora and fauna of the Arctic. The *Peary* led the *Bowdoin* through massive ice floes that would have trapped and crushed the schooner had she been alone.

It was while nuzzling her way through the growlers near Hopedale, Labrador, that the *Peary* "fetched up" for the first time in her life. Mariners sometimes call it "touching ground," but it was not ground, as we know it, but a tremendous and uncharted underwater chunk of granite, the kind called "sunkers" along the Labrador and Newfoundland coasts—deadly and immovable objects that have claimed many ships. Her forefoot hit sharply and unexpectedly, sliding up and ahead. But then she quickly reversed engines and withdrew with as much poise as she could muster. It was a blow that would have caused extensive and expensive repairs for any ship but the *Peary*. But her extra heavy shell plating and framing absorbed the blow with no apparent effect.

Ultimately the *Peary* was to learn much more of saltwater. She was to know intimately the vivid contrasts between life afloat in the frozen North and saltwater steaming as it is in the tropics.

Shortly after her Arctic adventures came to an end the

now famous *Peary* was sold to Matthew F. Bramley, million-aire head of the Trinidad Asphalt Company, the nation's largest paving contractors, headquartered in Cleveland where Bramley was Commodore of the Cleveland Yachting Club.

The *Peary* was enrolled at the Port of Cleveland under the sole ownership of Bramley, the provisions of the enroll-ment entitling the vessel to engage only in trade with foreign countries or with the Philippine Islands and the Island of Guam. It was under no circumstances to engage in the United States coastwise trade.

Bramley, who could afford his every pleasure, financed the Bramley–Carter Expedition whose ultimate goal, so their press releases stated, was the exploration of the Mayan ruins in Yucatan and a search for additional sites of cities swal-lowed up by the jungle. Colonel Charles Lindbergh had re-ported that the almost hidden cities could be seen from the air. Second in importance, (some say it was the compelling motivation) was the close study of Socorro Island, one of the uninhabited Revilla Gigedo group, about three hundred miles off the southern tip of California.

Bramley had made no secret of the fact that he hoped to buy Socorro Island from the Mexican government, there to establish his "Dream Island," which, under his direction, was to become a nation in itself. Another plan of Bramley's, or one that he intended to investigate, was the creation of an-other island by sinking barges on the outlines of a submerged coral reef and filling in the enclosed area with heavy material dredged up from the sea. It may be that the Socorro Island deal was just a diverting action while his engineers were determining the feasibility of building an island out of the coral formations. In either event, the chosen Dream Island site would, in Bramley's words, "become the prestige game fishing headquarters of the world." But when his engineers pointed out obstacles that could not be overcome, Bramley lost interest in both locations.

Included in the expedition were John C. Pallister, entomologist of the Cleveland Museum of Natural History, and Dr. George P. Englehardt, biologist of the Brooklyn Museum of Arts and Sciences. Other key figures in the proposed exploration program were James R. Carter and Arthur F. Morgan, friends of Bramley's, along with their wives. Carter was to send a series of progress stories to a Cleveland newspaper.

The *Peary,* after a stop at Chelsea, Massachusetts, where oil-burning equipment was installed in place of the coal-fired boilers, wended her way through the Panama Canal and up the Mexican and California coasts to Long Beach, where the members of the exploring party were gathering and checking equipment. The *Peary* was under the able command of Captain C. V. Griffin, a patient man who was to need all of his forbearance before the journey ended.

Off they started, on the last day of January, 1930. The first stop was at Socorro Island where, out of a larger party that started, two managed to scale the island's three-thousand foot Mount Evermann.

Next stop was San José, on the west coast of Guatemala, where the scientists had intended making a trip into the interior. But here the first of many complications developed and the collecting trips were postponed.

Now with the American Museum of Natural History in New York, entomologist John C. Pallister recalls the trip vividly. "Unfortunately," he says, "while Mr. Bramley was undoubtedly sincere, some of the others were not, which decided us at Balboa to cut the trip short and return home. I will not list all the bad things that happened. At one point the Captain threatened to throw some of those aboard into irons unless they behaved. As a result they were confined to the boat while she lay in Puerto Barrios harbor."

While the *Peary* was being repainted and provisioned and the roisterers confined to ship, Bramley; his nurse, a Miss Nugent; Dr. Englehardt; and Pallister went into the interior of Guatemala to visit a coffee plantation on the slopes of Mount Atilan. The plantation was owned by a brother of Dr. Englehardt. They stayed a month, while aboard the *Peary* the Carters and Morgans fretted in the heat of Puerto Barrios harbor.

After one more stop at Yucatan the ship set sail for Miami, where the expedition broke up. Pallister and Dr. Englehardt went south into the Everglades, and a relieved Captain Griffin prepared to take the *Peary* up the Atlantic Coast and down the St. Lawrence to Lake Erie, where new owners, the U.S. Coast and Geodetic Survey, waited anxiously to claim her.

Between the arctic and tropical expeditions, however, momentous happenings were taking place in Lake Superior, where the one-time minesweeper had first felt water under her keel. On a wonderfully calm June day in 1929 the U.S. Lake Survey vessel *Margaret* was making routine cross-lake line surveys, in Canadian waters, using an echo sounder to chart the depths. The recorded figures were much as anticipated—500, 800 and even 900 feet, a completely routine charting in supposedly known and previously charted waters. Captain Frank Green of the *Margaret* was holding a steady course as Harry F. Johnson, chief of the Lake Survey's offshore section, casually watched the graph on the echo sounder recording depths that varied between 400 and 800 feet. At the moment they were on the prescribed steamer track from the Soo to Ft. William and Port Arthur.

"Hold 'er a minute, Frank," shouted Johnson. "This

blasted echo sounder is acting funny. Went from 440 feet up to 50 feet and then back to 400."

To double check, Green turned the *Margaret* around and retraced his course. This time from 400 feet the graph pen zoomed up to 45 feet and then back to over 400 feet. Shoal water!

Quickly word was sent out to shipping interests, and all vessel masters were advised to avoid the area until further surveys could be made. The following year the Canadian Hydrographic Survey units made additional soundings and found a least depth of 22 feet.

Immediately named "Superior Shoal" and henceforth marked on all charts, the *Margaret*'s discovery resulted in entirely new recommended courses, the area being considered a menace to navigation in any weather. Situated nearly in the center of Lake Superior, the shoal is comprised of sharp mountain peaks that rise nearly to the surface. Strangely, too, commercial fishermen had apparently known about the shoal for years, for their nets were found all around the submerged peaks by the Canadian survey vessel *Bayfield*. The *Bayfield*'s probing lead lines hit the iron deck of one ship, fouled the rigging of another. The danger to shipping could not have gone unrecognized, and it is not to the credit of the fishermen that the shoal went unreported.

Quite likely then, on the hard slopes that slide quickly down to deep water, are the bones of the *Niagara, Manistee, Superior, Sunbeam, Merchant, Atlanta* and the minesweepers *Inkerman* and *Cerisolles*. True, on a calm day any one of them might have passed safely over Superior Shoal. But picture a ship in a gale, dropping 15 to 20 feet in the troughs of the seas. What then? Surely they would have been gutted as neatly as a herring on a fishmonger's bench. And in such catastrophic founderings there would be little wreckage, only an incredibly swift plunge to the bottom.

Meanwhile, the *Peary*, home from her saltwater wanderings, was being prepared for extensive offshore hydrographic work. New steel deckhouses were added and the ship fitted out with the latest type navigating and surveying gear including gyroscopic compass, radio direction finder and a new, improved sonic depth finder.

Also added was a complete outfit for "sweeping." In this operation a wire from 500 to 5000 feet long, depending on circumstances, is drawn between the steamer and a small launch, also part of the ship's equipment. The wire is suspended at the required depth from floats 100 feet apart, the entire length then being pulled over a given area. Any obstruction projecting above the depth at which the sweep is set will be caught by the wire and thus located. It was with the *Peary*'s sweeping gear that the wreck of the foundered steamer *Sand Merchant* was found in Lake Erie near Cleveland in 1936.

In 1941, before Pearl Harbor but when the war in Europe was fast making the industrialized lower lakes cities America's "Arsenal of Democracy," the U.S. Lake Survey, with permission of the Canadian authorities, embarked on a program of fully exploring and defining the Superior Shoal area.

It was even more important now to know the full extent of the granite masses that rose from the bottom of the lake, for the Great Lakes bulk trade, almost dormant in the Great Depression years of the 1930's, was now booming as all the industrial might of the nation was mustered to support the war with Hitler's Germany. Ships that had been laid up for ten years were fitted out and went puffing and creaking off on the iron ore shuttle from Lake Superior to the steel mills at the lower lakes ports. Many were available only because, during the years of their hibernation, it would have cost more to cut them up than they would have brought on the depressed scrap market. Not since the 1890's, when, because of their modest size, it took many more ships to carry the equivalent tonnage, had so many bottoms been put to work.

So once again the gallant old *Peary,* née *Rowena,* née *Bautzen,* tasted the cold blue of Lake Superior, where twenty-three years earlier she had been born and where even now the battered hulks of the *Inkerman* and *Cerisolles* and the bones of their crews lay just below her keel.

Sailors hold that each ship has a personality of her own. Even sister ships, those built from the same plans, develop individual characteristics and temperaments that sometimes differ significantly. Their stance, or "squat," when loaded, may vary; one may answer her helm briskly, the other listlessly. And they often show little similarity in their behavior in a seaway, one tending to be a little stiff, the other tender.

Above all, some maintain, a ship never stops talking, either to herself or her companions. Moored, she is forever grumbling as her hawsers squawk resentfully and her bitts offer high-pitched, rasping complaints. Under way she is extremely voluble. Plates and frames groan, her woodwork squeaks, her top hamper sings in the wind, her whistle bleats and her anchors chatter restlessly. It is the language of ships, supposedly heard and understood by other vessels whether they are afloat or on the bottom where, alas, there is naught to do but listen.

What, then, on this painfully touching reunion, would the *Peary* be saying to her lost companions of that great black, whistling gale of long ago?

"Ah, dear sisters—poor dear sisters. I have traveled far and witnessed much since that dreadful night when we met the storm and you met these terrible shoals. But I have come back to seek out and mark forever the granite peaks so that others may not suffer as you did—"

Slowly, with Captain Nimrod Long as her master and

William T. Laidly as the engineer in charge of the charting project, the *Peary* drew her sweep back and forth across the shoal waters. This time another submerged peak, with a diameter of 100 feet, was found within 21 feet of the surface. Only two cable lengths away the depth was 630 feet. The area of Superior Shoal considered dangerous in even a moderate sea, with vessels dropping 10 or 15 feet in the troughs is nearly one and one-half miles long. Other peaks, projecting upward like tiger's fangs, provide depths of only 28, 30 and 43 feet over their crests.

How many ships Superior Shoal claimed before being discovered can only be conjecture. But how else can one account for the complete disappearance of a score or more of merchantmen or, for that matter, the *Inkerman* and *Cerisolles?* The designers of the minesweepers knew that the very nature of their work would involve them in frequent jousts with rocks, shoals and old wrecks. But these encounters, during sweeping operations, would come while the ships were moving slowly in calm or moderate seas. They could never have envisioned plunging downward in the troughs of mountainous seas with express train speed only to strike on sharp unyielding granite peaks with such force that they would be instantly disemboweled.

Despite her eminently satisfactory work in charting the infamous shoals and in the myriad other tasks assigned her, there came a day, as there comes a day for all ships, when her practical life with the Lake Survey people came reluctantly to an end.

She was eventually acquired and registered as a steam yacht by a Mr. Glen L. Allen of Dearborn, Michigan. It was the beginning of hard and strange times for the *Peary,* eleven years of being shuttled from pillar to post, like an aged widow who has raised her brood only to find herself unwelcome at their doors.

In 1950 Allen resold her to John T. Cruickshank, master mariner, of Jollimore, Nova Scotia. In 1952 the *Peary* again changed hands, this time becoming the property of Orville Bates Pulsifer, of Halifax, who, a year later, transferred the title to Pulsifer Brothers, Limited. In less than a year she was acquired by the Peary Steamship Company, Limited, a firm that three months later surrendered title, again to Pulsifer Brothers, Limited. In two years she changed hands again, this time becoming the property of Sea Traders, Limited, also a Halifax firm. On January 19, 1961, she had her final change of ownership, this time to Dixon's Transportation, Limited, of Fortune Bay, Newfoundland.

Strangely, during the years when she was being bandied about like a pawn in a monstrous chess game, her name was never changed. She was alternately registered as a tug and a cargo vessel. Sea Traders, Limited, indicated that she was to be used as a seal-fishing vessel part of the time, a cargo ship in the off season. They also took out her old engine and boilers, replacing them with a modern diesel plant.

From a minesweeper to a steam yacht and from a survey boat to a tug and finally a humble cargo vessel, the forty-three-year-old *Peary* had known many lives and had changed, structurally, to adapt to each. She did it uncomplainingly, knowing perhaps that had she been built of less sturdy stock she would have long since felt the sting of the shipbreaker's torches.

She was still earning her keep that August day in 1961 when, burdened with 250 tons of salt fish, she sprang a leak some sixty miles west by north of St. Pierre Island. She went down slowly as her crew sought vainly the source of the incoming water. Luckily, they were picked up by the British motor vessel *Fergus* even before the *Peary* went down.

It took the Atlantic three hours to finish her, and one

wonders if, in her final agony, as she laid her head down on the bosom of the great Western Ocean, she could hear the voices of condolence from the *Inkerman* and *Cerisolles* in far-away Lake Superior—"Ah, dear sister . . . poor dear sister."

# 13

⚓

## *The Ice Committee*

From the upper-floor windows of Duluth's Board of Trade Building, where the shipping and grain office clerks were knotted, to the spacious lounge of the plush Kitchi Gammi Club out on Superior Street, where their superiors were wont to gather late of a working day, all eyes on that mild May afternoon of 1924 were riveted out over the miles of slush ice on Lake Superior. There the errant smoke streamers of eleven inbound vessels could be counted.

What had been a routine day in the affairs of the city's great shipping and brokerage fraternity had quite suddenly become a dramatic one. Shortly after noon the wind, fitful but from the west for days, swung rapidly around to the east and began to freshen. To those in other occupations the change probably went unnoticed. But to men who own, manage or charter ships, wind and ice form a detested partnership. The unholy alliance can play hob with schedules planned so carefully for weeks ahead. Now miles of slush ice, drifting willy-nilly over western Lake Superior for weeks, began to move in. As it gradually became confined by the narrowing shoreline of the fingerlike extremity of the lake, where Duluth lies at its very tip, the moving ice would begin to compact. Once it became "anchored" on the shore and began to pile up on Minnesota Point, it would further compact and deepen to become an almost impenetrable barrier.

The distant ships, black smoke now vomiting from their stacks as if each as an individual and every man aboard them sensed the urgency of the occasion, came charging on.

Would they make it? It is just such tense a situation that inspires men to venture knowing judgments and wager a dollar or two in support of them. So it was behind the leaded glass windows of the Kitchi Gammi Club, where prosperous ship owners, grain merchants and cargo brokers were laying their bets. The odds, perhaps influenced by the good fellowship and air of well-being that prevailed, were about even. But up in the Board of Trade Building, where the bets were more modest and the bettors much more realistic, the odds favored the ice, two to one.

Two days earlier the vessels had wended their way single file up the ice-choked St. Marys River and into open water near Isle Parisienne, steering around major accumulations of pack ice and nuzzling the smaller ones aside. And now, because they were relatively of the same size and graced with almost identical power plants, they were still strung out in parade formation, though, like weary marchers, somewhat out of step.

One of them was the steamer *Howard M. Hanna Jr.* Her captain, like the other skippers in the commercial flotilla, had noted the sudden change in the wind. Recalling previous occasions when his ship had been immobilized in slush ice under similar circumstances, he wanted no part of a repeat performance. Even though the engine order telegraph was already at "full ahead," he called the engine room, demanded extra revolutions and got them.

Masters of the other ships apparently shared his fears, for soon all eleven were driving ahead, as they say in naval circles, "under forced draft." Still, they could already feel increased resistance as the wind-driven ice began to build down from the surface. Even with their engines laboring at maximum power the pace was slowing to half speed with two miles still to go. A mile off Minnesota Point they were approximating "slow ahead" although the telegraphs still registered "full ahead." It was going to be nip and tuck or "brains and boilers," as the sailors term it, right down to the piers at the Duluth ship canal entrance!

Preceded by a smoke screen of their own making, the desperate line butted slowly ahead. When the leading ship was but a half mile from the piers it slowed to a halt, clutched from Plimsoll mark to keel in slush ice of the consistency of peanut butter. Resolutely the others came on, propellers thrashing furiously. Trying to find a path around their leader, they sheered starboard and port until they were all hopelessly scattered like jackstraws and stuck in a mass of ice that would have resisted the onward charge of a battleship!

Slush ice, as one sailor tried to explain it to a landlubber, "is the worstest kind."

When it extends well below the water line, as it does when compacted and displaced by a vessel, slush ice tends to move in to surround its victim, preventing movement in any direction. It damages propellers, mauls rudders and fills condenser intakes. It is indeed the "worstest" kind.

Eleven ships and three hundred men. Only a half-mile from shore but marooned as effectively as if they were icebound in polar seas. Day after day the wind continued to hold from the east, as if it knew no other compass point and would continue from the same direction for an eternity. Aboard the now submissive steamers, the *Howard M. Hanna*

*Jr.* in particular, the situation was growing more serious by the hour. The *Hanna* had taken on modest stores at her lower lakes unloading port, intending to provision again at Duluth. Now, after nearly two weeks in the ice, the meat locker had been barren for days, the canned stock devoured and the eggs and flour almost gone.

"Tomorrow," grinned the steward, "we're going to have a fine old sailor's stew—hatch tarpaulins and old work gloves with a little capstan grease to make it stick to your ribs." The humor was lost on first mate Henry F. Wiersch, who had been in a mood of seething frustration for a week.

The Wiersches lived in Duluth, and Henry (his friends call him "Heinie"), peering through his binoculars, could see his wife leave the house with her shopping bag every morning and watch her come home with it loaded with groceries.

"All I can think of is the good things to eat in that shopping bag," he groaned to a shipmate. "Right now I could eat the gaskets out of the pumps."

Fortunately, before the steward could resort to his threatened stew, the wind swung around to the southwest. In only a few hours the ice was gone, again a pawn of the wind and water. Whistles sobbing their vast relief, the eleven long-beset freighters steamed humbly to their assigned docks.

It was over two years before Heinie got really hungry again, the fall of 1926, to be specific.

There were a great number of ships in Lake Superior during the last days of November that year. In the Canadian ports of Ft. William and Port Arthur they were loading grain at a record pace, and at Duluth, Ashland, Two Harbors and Marquette the booming of ore in the loading chutes was like thunder over the north country. Out they went, one after another, under sullen skies, headed for the Soo. It was one of the coldest Novembers on record. Out on the lake, ship masters looked incredulously at thermometers that registered

25, 30, even 35 degrees below zero. And they knew what such weather would do at the St. Marys River and the locks.

Telegraphs stayed at "full ahead" despite seas that were exploding over the bows and cascading over the cabins, fore and aft. A coating of ice rimmed every hull, growing thicker by the moment. But ice on the ships was the lesser of two evils now. It was a race to get to the Soo and out of the St. Marys before the ships became prisoners for the winter. Billowing black smoke from their funnels, flattened and dissipated by gale force winds, lay like unmistakable evidence of panic all along the horizon.

> When the skies grow gray
> And the wind blows free;
> Batten down the hatches,
> Come below with me.
>
> If it's twenty at Duluth
> And ten at Marquette,
> It's zero at the Soo
> And colder it will get.
>
> When the seas are on the deck
> And the rails icy, too;
> Keep up your courage,
> We're almost at the Soo.
>
> When there's ice in the compass,
> Clinkers in the stew;
> Look lively mates,
> I think I see the Soo.
>
> The captain's got a bearing
> On old Stannard Rock.
> In twenty hours, boys,
> We'll be sittin' at the dock.

Below Whitefish Point the ice was already building from the shore as the converging steamers came abreast of Point

Iroquois and slipped gratefully into single file, most of them
resembling icebergs. The *W. E. Fitzgerald* had picked up
1200 tons of ice on her hull.

Hooting impetuously, the great armada locked through
with clocklike regularity, falling into line again below the
locks, where rafting ice had begun to find its way into the
channel. For several miles, as though playing follow-the-
leader, they wended their way along the historic course,
where only a few feet from the spar decks the pines stood
straight and tall. Suddenly, however, there was no place to
go. One of the leading vessels, sheering her steering chains,
had struck hard aground along the twisting channel. In the
confusion of the moment, as whistles bellowed, telegraph
bells rang and orders were shouted, her stern had swung
broadside in the river, plugging it like a bung in a barrel.
Behind her, anchors thundering down in panic, two hundred fifty steamers dragged themselves to a stop.

The temperature fell to thirty-five below that night, and
by dawn the river was frozen solid. Two tugs had bulled
their way down from the Soo overnight, but theirs was a
hopeless task. The ship they could move but not the untold
tons of encompassing ice that beset her and the great fleet
upriver.

A week went by, then ten days. The temperature rarely
climbed above twenty degrees below zero. The ice on the
river, solid for days now and getting thicker by the hour, was
black from the soot of two hundred fifty smoking funnels.
By day a forest of masts marked the wavering channel, like
a straggling picket line of sentinels watching hopefully for
help that might, or might not, come. At night the river came
abloom with lights where before had been only the lonely
pines and dark water.

Galley stocks were about gone. Stewards trudged over the
ice making swaps with galley skippers of other vessels. Still,

meals were, of necessity, becoming somewhat skimpy. Farmers and Indians had built up a thriving trade, sledding out to the stranded fleet with tobacco, maple syrup and chickens, but the supply was not enough.

By this time Heinie, now first mate of the *John A. Topping*, was getting hungry again. This was hard sheet ice, not pack ice, and he could do something about it. Early one morning he enlisted the aid of a small shore party of volunteers. They trudged several miles in the direction of a farmhouse he had spotted with his binoculars.

"Where there's a farm, there's food," he promised the crew.

The contented lowing of cattle in the barn quickened their pace as they neared the house.

The farmer was no fool. He sensed desperation and recognized a seller's market when it came trudging to his door. The commodity in question was an ordinary-looking cow that viewed the intruders with innocent eyes. Her owner, extolling her many virtues and distinguished lineage, drove a hard bargain. But Heinie and his men were more interested in her flavor than her ancestry, and after some haggling the deal was consummated and the beast slain on the spot.

"Come to think of it, that was a darn fool thing to do," Heinie reminisces. "Carrying a dead cow, even in pieces, over five or six miles of ice was plain crazy. We could have walked her back to the ship and killed her there."

Luckily, before the shore party had to return for another cow, one of the big Straits of Mackinac car-ferries fought her way up from Detour. She cut a swath around the grounded vessel, pulled her free and then charged up the river to free the fleet. Strident whistles welcoming their release, the long freighters went snoring out into Lake Huron and home for the winter.

Heinie Wiersch was a captain for many years and then

marine superintendent for the Columbia Transportation fleet before retiring to Florida. But even basking in the sun at Pompano Beach, the poignant memories of those frustrating ordeals in the ice still make him shudder.

Inescapably, if they are to enjoy a full season and prosperity, Great Lakes ships have always had to battle ice. It is one of the forces over which the most astute captain or knowledgeable fleet manager has no control. Wind-driven ice is an implacable and unpredictable foe. No scientist can calculate the tremendous pressures exerted by miles of floe or sheet ice marching ominously before the wind. Hundreds of sailing ships have been wrecked or shredded, reduced to kindling while they lay helpless in its grasp. Yet today's steamer, though it has the ability to claw away from encroaching ice fields rapidly, is an even more subservient victim once it is surrounded. Lacking the resilience of the old wooden hulls, the plates crack and the frames bend. And they do not spring back in place when shifting winds ease the pressure.

Far from shore, some of the great dramas of the Great Lakes have taken place unnoticed by all but the sailors involved, the shipping agents who had to account for the cargoes and the insurance underwriters and surveyors who tallied the cost. And the situation changed little when steam replaced sail.

In the 1890's nine schooners, all carrying grain cargoes, were trapped in the center of a huge island of pack and slush ice in Lake Erie. For over two dreary weeks they lay silent and forlorn while their white island moved lazily at the will of the winds. One night they would drift in nearly to the Canadian shore. Dawn might find them just off Dunkirk, New York. East and west they went, too, from Cleveland to within sight of Buffalo harbor. Food supplies were exhausted, and the last of the wood for their stoves went up in smoke.

Chairs, bunks, shifting boards, washstands and cabin paneling were chopped up and grudgingly fed to the demanding stoves. When the last morsel of food had been devoured the cooks broached the cargoes, pounding up wheat into a mash from which they made highly unpalatable hotcakes. Barley soup was plentiful if not popular.

Aboard the *Dunkirk Lass,* old Captain Harley Morton was hard put to maintain order and discipline. After a steady diet of wheat-mash cakes and barley soup, sailors took to conversing in high-pitched whinnys. There was talk of skating the ship's yawl over the ice to open water. On other occasions the master detected what he thought were covetous glances directed toward his pet dog. Thereafter he took to pacing the deck with the dog on a leash and a pistol in his pocket.

> We burned the captain's chair,
> Legs, back and stuffin' hair.
> Go get our cookie's bunk.
> Now we need another chunk.

Eventually a modest gale dispersed the ice, and the schooners put into Erie to replenish their larders. Ironically, over a half century later, on May 10, 1947, thirty-six big steamers were hopelessly locked in the ice off Buffalo. Four years earlier, during World War II, the same situation prevailed in the same area. When food ran low, planes parachuted supplies to the stranded vessels. At night the lights of many ships twinkled and flickered in the dusk where in summer only blue water and the hazy shoreline of Ontario are visible.

Captain Wiersch was long a part of the annual battle with the ice, and that is probably why, when he came ashore as marine superintendent, he served willingly and ably on the advisory group of the Ice Committee, a unique executive group in American industry.

Every year, at approximately ten o'clock on a late February morning, the Ice Committee and its associated advisory group foregather in a somewhat somber board room in Cleveland's Rockefeller Building. They will meet weekly, sometimes oftener, until the need for their unusual function no longer exists, probably in about five or six weeks.

The Ice Committee of the Lake Carriers' Association is concerned with exactly what the name indicates—the hundreds of miles of ice that close the shipping lanes of the Great Lakes for the winter. They represent the Association's twenty-four members, operating 226 big bulk freighters.

Officially six in number, usually managing directors of shipping firms, they are augmented by a staff of specialists—shore captains, marine superintendents, the chief meteorologist of the Cleveland Weather Bureau, the commander of the Ninth District (Great Lakes) of the United States Coast Guard, personnel of the U.S. Army Corps of Engineers and often local representatives of Canadian shipping companies.

Primarily the Ice Committee's responsibility is to determine the earliest possible date when the shipping lanes and harbors of the upper lakes can be broken out. It is not entirely an arbitrary decision, for it is one in which the Coast Guard, which must implement the ice-breaking operations, must concur. It is a date which, after all known factors are considered, is consistent with the safety of the vessels and the men who sail them.

Like generals with the profile of a continent before them, they rely heavily on "intelligence reports" that never show on the charts but often swing the balance of decision.

Perhaps the most knowledgeable and revealing data on which the Ice Committee dwells at length comes from a small army of volunteer "ice reporters," one hundred twenty of them stationed at strategic points in Canada and the United States. It is part of a massive ice-reporting program operated by the Detroit Weather Bureau. Fishermen, pilots, schoolteachers, storekeepers, businessmen and even a post-mistress, each with an intimate knowledge of the ice charac-teristics of his or her particular area, forward data regularly. These are some of the intelligence operatives—people who chop holes in the ice, measure it, observe it knowingly and watch through binoculars for pressure ridges and windrows.

More ice data come regularly from lonely Coast Guard stations, airline pilots and other agencies. Ice is gauged for thickness, extent of coverage, amount of windrowing and degree of deterioration. All this information is correlated in weekly bulletins until the lakes and their connecting chan-nels once more resound to the sobs of steamer whistles. Special reports from critical areas are subject to coverage in daily teletype bulletins.

In March the ice reporting is intensified. Coast Guard planes scout the lakes, noting the extent of shore-fast ice and drifting ice fields and observing the humping and windrowing. Far out on Whitefish Bay one of its helicopters flutters down on the sheet ice. Crews drill holes, measure the thickness and report to Cleveland. And always, the chief meteorologist's long-range projected weather report for the coming weeks is a vital factor, bearing heavily on the strat-egy being evolved.

Actually, two dates are involved. One is for breaking out the Straits of Mackinac, connecting Lake Huron and Lake Michigan and freeing the ice-beset harbors of both lakes. The other date is that of the much more difficult campaign to open up the winding St. Marys River to the locks at Sault Ste. Marie and then on up from the Soo to infamous White-fish Bay and Lake Superior. This has become known as the "big push" and, ironically, it is often in full swing when in lower lakes cities crowds are flocking to the opening baseball games. And sometimes when the baseball season is two or three weeks old the lake freighters will still be slugging it out with their old enemy—ice!

Winter comes early to the Soo and Lake Superior country. This is the land of the Chippewas, of Hiawatha and of Gitche Gumee—the shining Big-Sea-Water. A hundred years ago it was a little known land of mystery and Indian legends. To-day, if one could but lay open the economic anatomy of America, it is, from Detour to Whitefish Point, the 86-mile coronary artery that links the fabulously productive iron ore country of upper Michigan, Wisconsin and Minnesota to the blast furnaces of the industrialized Midwest.

In a single year during World War II, Great Lakes ships moved 194 million tons of critical commodities on the lakes, including 92 million tons of iron ore. In 1953 they carried 215 million tons, 95 million of which were iron ore.

In the eight-, sometimes nine-month shipping season the fleets of deep-bellied freighters must carry enough ore to last the furnaces for twelve. The shipping men know, from individual vessel capacities and average trips-per-ship-per-season records, exactly what their annual potential is. But that potential shrinks several hundred thousand long tons for every week the fleets are delayed at the start of the season. And when the potential approaches the estimated consumer demand for steel for the coming year, an early start becomes an economic necessity.

Armed with these hard statistics, the shippers are, however, always cognizant of the fact that variables of weather can often upset their plans. During World War I, with ore in critical demand, heavy floe ice plugged many Lake Superior harbors throughout the month of May. In June a strong northeast gale jammed the ice so tightly into Duluth harbor that a score of vessels were unable to clear the loading docks. When finally released, the same vessels reported dangerous rafted ice in Whitefish Bay. And this in June!

When the ice is done there is often fog. It descends in an almost impenetrable shield that stops traffic at the locks and all along the St. Marys River. Long ships lay stewing at anchor. Hour by hour others join them, creeping at "slow ahead" while seeking safe anchorage. Each with whistle sounding once every minute, the prescribed fog signal, they lie there bellowing like impatient bullfrogs meeting in convention and anxious to get on with it. But the Coast Guard controls the river traffic, and word to proceed must come from their "Soo Control."

These are the things the men who make up the loading and sailing schedules cannot possibly predict. Therefore there must be an elasticity of movement. If the ore-unloading docks of one port are jammed and the incoming vessel faces a long wait, its master can quickly be reached by radiotelephone to divert his ship to another port.

One of the trump cards the Coast Guard holds in the annual effort to stretch the season is its big icebreaker *Mackinaw*. *"Big Mac,"* the lake sailors call her, a burly, broad-beamed, 10,000-horsepower monster built during World War II to do just what she has been doing ever since—lead the "big push" up to Lake Superior. Others refer to her as the "rock and roll" ship, a tribute to her unique ability to shift water ballast quickly from one side to the other to literally rock herself out of difficulties. She is built to plow up onto heavy sheet ice, crushing down through it as her bow propeller sucks the water support from beneath it. *Big Mac* was designed by the Coast Guard's Admiral Edward H. Thiele, who also designed other of the nation's newest and largest saltwater icebreakers.

In 1957 the "battle of the ice" was typical. It was easier than some years, tougher than others. Waiting a couple of weeks would have eased the ice problem, but the economy was booming and the ore stockpiles had dwindled alarmingly.

An early start was indicated—if the projected weather report seemed favorable, if the ice accumulation had undergone any degree of deterioration and if contrary winds did not, in moments, continually make a mockery of the icebreaking task force by closing the leads they opened. For a number of shipmasters in the vessels fitting out, the situation seemed far too iffy. And a few had no qualms about saying so.

In early March the intelligence reports from the ice reporters and personal flights over Lake Superior by shipping officials seemed to reveal that deterioration in most areas was sufficient to warrant a try. March 18 was established for the first assault on the ice in the Straits of Mackinac and the upper Lake Michigan and Lake Huron ports. The "big push" up through the Soo would begin on April 5.

In Cleveland Admiral Thiele and his chief-of-staff, Captain Oliver A. Peterson, made their plans. Together, they had spent most of their service life fighting ice and devising new methods of combating it. Captain Peterson once commanded the famous Greenland Patrol and was skipper of the Coast Guard Cutter *Eastwind* when it made the closest approach to the North Pole by a vessel under its own power.

By late March the *Mackinaw* had already spent three weeks breaking out the Straits, Green Bay, Grand Traverse Bay and the iron ore port of Escanaba. She had also bulled open Lake Huron's Saginaw Bay and the ports of Alpena and Rogers City, from where fleets of self-unloading vessels supply the limestone needs of the lower lakes steel centers.

Now came the toughest job of all—smashing a path up the St. Marys and into Lake Superior. It called for all the heavy-duty craft the Coast Guard could muster. *Big Mac* led a task force of six Coast Guard vessels into the fray. The *Arundel, Kaw, Sundew, Acacia, Woodbine* and *Mesquite* are primarily cutters and buoy tenders, but all have specially reinforced, ice-breaking bows. They were joined by the large carferry *Sainte Marie,* almost as broad as the *Mackinaw* and a veteran of forty years of breaking ice in the Straits of Mackinac.

Commanding the task force from the bridge of the *Big Mac* was Captain Evor S. Kerr. From Detour they ranged north and into the ice. *Big Mac* was smashing down thirty-six-inch ice without slowing her progress. The shock sent great cracks out port and starboard, and the booming of the shattering ice echoed far up the river. Behind churned the *Arundel, Sundew, Acacia, Woodbine, Mesquite* and *Kaw,* breaking up the large floes created by their leader. Still farther behind came the *Sainte Marie,* widening the original "cut" and breaking up the sheet ice in the winding bends where the lake ships swing wide in making their turns. Some of the broken ice would be carried out into the North Channel and Lake Huron by the current and prevailing winds. Most of it would still be in the river for weeks, creating trouble spots as it compacted and froze again in pressure ridges.

Leading interference, the Coast Guard task force preceded a convoy of some one hundred freighters, their snoring whistles and the thunder of breaking ice signaling another year of commerce for the Soo country.

The Coast Guard maintains strict control over all vessel movements in the St. Marys, and from its Soo Control, at Saulte Ste. Marie, directs progress of the individual vessels. On a huge plot board, magnetized cutouts depict the passage of each ship in the ice armada. The big-muscled, 5000-horsepower steamers are the advance troops, those with lower indicated horsepower follow in their wake.

There were ominous tidings of what lay ahead. The *Big Mac*'s helicopter reported the Lake Superior ice field extending some fifty miles beyond Whitefish Point. And Whitefish Bay, the pilots said, was a nightmare of ice. . . . slush, floe and the flat, hard, blue type, the latter broken up into windrows by the pressure of winter gales, into compacted hills as high as the icebreaker's flying bridge.

"Hold 'em where they are," Captain Kerr told Commander Elmer J. Bodenlos, in charge of Soo Control.

Commander Bodenlos, by radio-telephone, ordered the freighter convoy to anchor in the river while Captain Kerr led his vessels into combat. Day after day, laboring around the clock, *Big Mac* punched ahead into the frozen hills. She would hit, reel back and hit again. Great towers would shear off the compacted ridges, crashing down to where the ice-breaker would smash them on her next charge. The leads she and the *Sainte Marie* battered open would close behind them, only to be opened again by the smaller cutters.

After weary days of pulverizing the ice in the channel and when he considered limited operations possible, Captain Kerr ordered a small convoy of freighters into single file behind the icebreaker. Following closely, stem to fantail, the first six vessels were led to open water.

For two days the *Mackinaw* continued her shuttle from the locks out to blue water, until all the ships were clear of ice and under power.

"Worst I've seen in fifty years," a grizzled ship captain was heard to comment to a skipper friend over the radio-telephone.

"They say that every year," grinned Captain Kerr.

Actually, the battle had barely commenced. Downbound from Duluth was a sizable convoy of ore-laden ships. *Big Mac* met them in open water far out in the lake. But the "lead" she had battered out for the upbound ships had long since been jammed shut by the pressure of more ice being driven in from the lake.

It was now April 16, and excerpts from the *Big Mac*'s log better tell the story of the ice battle of 1957:

16 April:

11:45 . . . *S. S. George A. Sloan,* under downbound escort by car-ferry *Sainte Marie,* in heavy ice six miles northwest of Isle Paris-ienne, reported herself taking water into forward stowage com-partments through cracks in hull plating. . . . *Mackinaw,* then assisting with escort of the *Hood* and *Dickson,* about one mile ahead, immediately assumed escort of *Sloan.* . . . ice conditions 90 percent icebreaking in heavy fields and floes, 18 to 20 inches thick. . . . *Sloan* then followed the *Mackinaw* into open lead. . . . *Sloan* reported pumps to be holding flooding. . . .

12:28 . . . priority arrangements were made to lock *Sloan* through the Soo when escort completed. . . .

13:15 . . . Just as *Sloan* entered ice again, she reported flooding too rapid to risk any further escort through ice. . . . ship backed into open water. . . . *Mackinaw* calls away salvage party . . . master of *Sloan* headlong for Northwest shore of Isle Parisienne in attempt to beach vessel. . . .

13:50 . . . *Mackinaw* boats numbers five and six away with sal-vage party and equipment. . . .

14:00 . . . *CGC Woodbine* alongside and away with Command-ing Officer, *Mackinaw,* as salvage master. . . . *Sloan* has bow in shorefast ice 0.3 miles offshore. . . . *Sloan* making preparations to abandon ship. . . .

Headed by Captain Kerr, the salvage crew boarded the stricken *Sloan.* Damage control officer Lieutenant Charles F. Baker, damage control chief Elmer Berrish, engineman Robert H. Lange and damage controlman Eugene Williams, all from the *Mackinaw,* were joined by damage controlman David F. Krenke of the *Woodbine* and engineman chief Edward F. Mattingly of the *Acacia.* Captain Thomas F. Har-bottle, representing the Lake Carriers' Association aboard the *Mackinaw,* was one of the first to board the *Sloan.* They found heavy flooding. The lower of the two compartments aft of the peak tank was filled, and the upper compartment flooded to within one foot of the overhead. The matter was compounded by a leaking personnel hatch in the upper compartment, which was permitting a large flow of water to pour down in the Number One cargo hold.

While Berrish, Williams, Krenke and Lange were feverishly constructing a temporary patch of rope yarn, caulking and mattresses, Captain Kerr, Lieutenant Baker and engineman chief Mattingly were calling over big 500-gallons per minute pumps from *Mackinaw* and *Woodbine*. *Acacia* hurriedly swung over another.

14:08 . . . Damage to *Sloan* extensive . . . ice cakes found in flooded upper compartments. . . . *W. C. Richardson,* equipped with bucket cranes, engaged to lighter the *Sloan's* cargo, proceeding upbound from Detour anchorage. . . . steamer *Eugene P. Thomas,* escorted by *Sainte Marie,* arrived to take the *Sloan's* lightered cargo. . . .
14:15 . . . *Woodbine* moored alongside and pumps from *Mackinaw* and *Woodbine* placed in operation. . . . *Acacia* moored alongside and dispatched additional salvage personnel with additional pump. . . . *Sloan* down by the head, drawing 26 feet of water forward. . . . submersible pump placed in No. 1 hold. . . .

17 April:
02:00 . . . *Richardson* and *Thomas* on scene, unloading. . . . *Mackinaw* broke off to engage in icebreaking along edges of fields threatening to move in on nested salvage vessels as winds shifted. . . .
14:36 . . . forepeak and dunnage compartments and number one hold of *Sloan* pumped out, revealing bow damage on both sides, two holes covering area two by six feet on starboard and five holes covering area two by fifteen feet on port side. . . . adjoining area of plating weakened. . . . damage control party welded patches in place and caulked and shored. . . . inside, the patches were caulked and shored, backed up by a soft patch and more shoring. . . .

18 April:

11:15 . . . salvage operations completed and vessel determined to be in safe condition to proceed. . . . fog set in, reducing visibility . . . departure delayed. . . .

15:00 . . . *Mackinaw* and *Woodbine* commenced escort to Saulte Ste. Marie. . . . salvage party returned to *Mackinaw*. . . . *Woodbine* released from task to resume escort of upbound convoy at 16:30. . . .

20:00 . . . *Sloan* arrived at the Soo locks. . . .

Three days later the *Mackinaw* again broke off convoy duty to rush to the aid of the steamer *Elbert R. Gary*, stricken as was the *Sloan*, with bow plates punched in by the ice. Again the salvage crews pumped and patched until the *Gary* was seaworthy enough to proceed to a port where permanent repairs could be made.

These ship-saving salvage operations, for which Captain Kerr and the salvage crews received official commendations, occurred, ironically, on days when in cities a few hundred miles to the south forsythia was in full flower, daffodils were in bloom and hopeful gardeners were planting early peas.

The big push and the long struggle it prompts becomes almost a personal vendetta that is renewed every year with no less determination. It is witnessed only by those whose duties bring them there. But among them are those who still remember the days when there wasn't an Ice Committee, before there was a *Big Mac* to break a path and succor the wounded. They know too that under the icy battlefield are the twisted plates and rotting ribs of countless other ships that came too soon or too late. Outside the great freshwater shipping fraternity they serve so valiantly, the labors of *Big Mac* and her sisters will go largely unheralded.

It is understandable then, when the annual battle of the ice is over, that *Big Mac,* her paint scarred and plates scored, gets a hearty "well done" whistle salute from every big freighter she meets. It is the greatest honor she and her crew are ever likely to get.

And it is the only kind they really care about.

# 14

⚓

# *Of Bones and Men*

In an era when 700-foot freighters are fast becoming the rule rather than the exception, it is perhaps somewhat incongruous but entirely fitting that in recent years scholars and researchers have devoted much time to one of the smallest Great Lake ships, the tiny barque *Griffon* and the tragic saga of her only voyage.

While but a scant fifty or sixty tons burden, although even her size and tonnage are debatable in historical circles, the *Griffon* was important for two reasons. She was, if one excepts the canoes and bateaux of the early explorers and traders, the first commercial craft to sail the lakes. Then, too, in recording some of the more enigmatic and baffling chapters of Great Lakes shipping from the first sloops and schooners to the thundering big freighters destined to follow them, it is significant to note that the *Griffon,* quite prophetically as it developed, chose to "go missing" on her first voyage.

One would suppose that the ancient *Griffon,* like hundreds of her larger successors who likewise mysteriously vanished, would long since have been forgotten in subsequent years of unparalled progress. Yet today, almost three hundred years since she "sailed away," the historic ship whose probable fate has come to light only in recent years is still an enigma . . . just as she has been since a September day in 1679 when she went scudding up Lake Michigan, past the hazy blue Beaver Islands only to meet a westerly gale and be driven before it into the Straits of Mackinac and eternity!

The remains of two ancient hulls, weathered by decades of ice, heat, frost, sun, storm and alternating periods of high and low water have been found, and each has been presumed and authenticated, to varying degrees, as the hallowed and long lost bones of the *Griffon*. Two camps of enthusiasts, each guided by sincere and devoted historians, have advanced data to justify their beliefs.

One wreck site is on the craggy western tip of Manitoulin Island, in Georgian Bay, far up on Lake Huron. The other, eighty-odd miles away, is located on Russell Island, off the tip of Ontario's Bruce Peninsula, also in Georgian Bay and near the town of Tobermory. Wreckage at the Russell Island site, and there was precious little, has since been removed for safekeeping to Tobermory. From the proposed homeward route of the *Griffon* either site would be an entirely logical grave for an undermanned vessel driven before fall gales and wracked by overpowering seas.

But in examining the facts, such as they are—and here again, since no building plans of the *Griffon* have ever been discovered and only the words of a scholarly friar remain to tell us of her construction—even the historians must rely, in many cases, upon their knowledge of early ship-building, probability and reasonable supposition.

Rene Robert Cavalier, Sieur de la Salle, began the building of the *Griffon* late in the winter, actually late January of 1679, near where Cayuga Creek empties into the Niagara River, well above the falls and not far from Lake Erie. La Salle had earlier built four small sloops on Lake Ontario, but they were mostly for ferrying supplies and materials across the lake for the building of a fort on the Niagara. Now the ambitious explorer wanted a really substantial vessel to explore the wild shores of the upper lakes, at the same time acquiring by trade and barter enough furs to bolster his sagging fortunes. Like so many of the great men whose names have since been written indelibly in history, La Salle was only partially subsidized by his king, existing and advancing for the most part by nimble wits, shrewd dealings, barter and promises. What little is known of the difficulties of the wilderness shipyard and the ship's first voyage comes from the pen of the expedition's spiritual counselor and chronicler, Friar Louis Hennepin. His words, seemingly a routine account of the building and sailing, have since been seized upon and variously interpreted by historians, who even now study the weathered timbers of the two wrecks in an effort to identify one or the other as that of the true *Griffon.*

The friar spoke of the felling of native white oak, the forging of ironwork, the solemn moment when La Salle himself drove home the bolt that held sternson and keel together and of the thrilling launching. Carved griffon, half eagle, half lion, marked the prow and stern of the vessel.

"High above the black crows shall the gallant griffon soar," La Salle is reported to have cried as the ship hit the water.

Sailing on August 6, 1679, according to Hennepin, the *Griffon* ranged cautiously the length of Lake Erie, narrowly averting disaster at Long Point and later among the many islands and shoals near its western end. The friar wrote glowingly and at length about the wondrous lush shores along what is now the Detroit and St. Clair rivers and of a terrible storm that fell upon them in Lake Huron, off Thunder Bay.

In the *Griffon* La Salle had a strangely assorted company of thirty-four—saints and sinners, scoundrels and scholars, soldiers of fortune, Franciscan friars, schemers and brandy traders. Of the regular crew, all of which were more than a year in arrears on their promised wages, one stands out, not only for his unusual physical measurements but for the key role historians feel he may have played in the vessel's eventual fate. He was La Salle's heretic Danish sailing-master or pilot Luke, sometimes called "Luke the Dane." A full seven feet tall and equally impressive in other dimensions, Luke was a truculent, quarrelsome individual given to disrespect to his superiors, scorn for the men of the cloth and violent physical action when he felt that discipline was needed among his subordinates. But he was a good pilot, and as he, like the others, had been unpaid for twelve months, the leader was obliged to keep him on.

Before reaching her destination at what is now Green Bay, off Lake Michigan's western shores, the ship stopped briefly at Michilimackinac, in the Straits of Mackinac, late in August before feeling her way cautiously through the maze of islands that dot upper Lake Michigan and that still plague mariners today.

Here La Salle hastily loaded the ship with beaver skins, instructing Luke and a crew of five to take her straight back to Niagara, where emissaries of his creditors clamored for the money due them. She was to return, so Hennepin related, with equipment for another ship with which La Salle hoped to explore the Mississippi. The explorer himself, with fourteen men, started for a point near what is now Peoria, Illinois, where the intended ship was to be built.

From a high point near Death's Door, one of the many

treacherous passages into Green Bay, Friar Hennepin saw the *Griffon* sail away. And later, armed with information from Indians who had encountered the ship, he took pen in hand at a point where the perplexing mystery begins.

Wrote Hennepin:

They sailed the 18th of September with a westerly wind. . . . The ship came to an anchor to the north of the lake of the Illinois [Lake Michigan] where she was seen by some Savages, who told us that they advised our men to sail along the coast and not towards the middle of the lake, because of the sands that make the navigation dangerous when there is any high wind. Our pilot [Luke] as I said before, was dissatisfied and would steer where he pleased, without hearkening to the advice of the Savages who, generally speaking, have more sense than the Europeans think at first; but the ship was hardly a league from the coast when it was tossed up by a violent storm in such a manner that our men were never heard of since; and it is supposed that the ship struck upon some sand and was there buried!

Actually, La Salle had given Luke an almost impossible task. With the equinox coming on and bringing with it, as always, heavy fall gales, the five men allotted him were not enough to work the ship in heavy weather, let alone man the seven cannon on board should the vessel be attacked by hostile Indians or the fur pirates who roamed the freshwater seas!

Luke, as some historians hold, must have realized this but made no strong protest (which surely would have been the case had he followed his usual inclinations), simply because he never intended to complete the journey or deliver the cargo! In such an event it would likely be some quiet bay or lagoon like that on Russell Island where the angry pilot and his crew would beach the vessel and plunder the cargo. Their wages unpaid, they might, in their own way of thinking, be justified in such action to get what they felt was their just due. It is also possible, quite probable in fact, that the Indians of the area would, over the years that followed, have stripped the vessel of her precious ironwork, burning or cutting away sections above water to make it accessible. Ice and the wearing action of the centuries of wind and water might then reduce the wreckage to the 40-foot keel and rib sections recovered by commercial fisherman Orrie C. Vail.

La Salle himself later viewed some evidence that the *Griffon* had perished in a gale. At St. Ignace he was shown wreckage—jetsam thrown upon the beach on Mackinac Island, in Lake Huron—a hatch cover, a cabin door, a few bundles of beaver skins and two pairs of breeches. All these suggest an overwhelming and violent end, although, with the exception of the beaver pelts, which would have been properly stowed deep in her hold, and the breeches, which should have been on the loins of two crew members, these bits of wreckage could have been carried away in a gale and the ship still survive. La Salle himself leaned heavily to the theory that Luke had inspired the crew to acts of barratry and that they, after disposing of the pelts to fur traders, had scuttled the ship in deep water.

As months went by the possibility of a successful attack by Indians was ruled out largely because Indians could not keep secrets. Notorious braggarts, they would have found it impossible to refrain from boasting of possession of her guns, her ironwork or the cargo of beaver pelts. Word would have leaked out somehow and somewhere, no matter what. The fact that the wreckage was found on Mackinac Island, well out in Lake Huron, indicated that the ship, although in the grip of a heavy gale, had somehow miraculously escaped stranding and had been driven through the Straits of Mackinac into Lake Huron. There the journey apparently ended, even as the mystery now deepens.

In the years since the *Griffon*'s disappearance there have

been no fewer than a dozen reports of the discovery of her bones. Only two, those related earlier in this chapter, have any substance of historical evidence. First to be examined is the wreck that could likely have lain on the rocky beach of Manitoulin Island, gateway to the Mississagi Strait, alone and unidentified for well over two centuries.

White settlers came late to Canada's lonely Manitoulin, the first in about 1862. The western tip of the island was virtually ignored as a likely area for farming until the 1880's. Present day residents recall yarns their grandfathers used to spin around warm kitchen stoves on winter nights, stories of the early pioneers who hacked away at the old wreck to get iron bolts that they forged into harrow teeth and of fishermen who set fires to release the lead caulking to mold into fishing weights. There was evidence even then, from the testimony of old Indians, that earlier generations of the red men had pillaged the wreck for its ironwork.

Regrettably then, important artifacts, perhaps conclusive evidence, were unthinkingly destroyed or lost long before the historians and researchers of today began their probing. The early settlers were much more concerned with the necessity of making a living at fishing or farming than identifying the pile of weathered timbers and rusty iron that lay on their beach. They knew little and cared less of a ship named *Griffon*.

Perhaps the most important discovery at Manitoulin was made shortly before the turn of the present century, although it was not considered particularly significant at the time. Lighthouse keeper William Cullis and his assistant John Holdsworth were clambering along the rocky shore near the wreck searching for a straight tree from which to fashion a boat mast. They startled a white rabbit, which immediately dove into a convenient hole. Holdsworth began to dig him out, soon finding that the hole was actually the almost completely filled entrance to a large niche or cave in the rock layers. He had scarcely begun to dig when he unearthed a large dark disc that, upon closer examination, proved to be an old silver watch case. Both excited now, they soon enlarged the opening and crawled cautiously inside. There they found six skeletons, exactly the number of the *Griffon's* crew!

On the stone floor lay several French coins, and a later search by Jack Allen, another assistant at the lighthouse, yielded nearly enough brass buttons to fill a baking powder can. Still another skeleton was found nearby at a later date, but because it had once been wrapped in birch bark it was presumed to be that of an Indian. Cave burials had earlier been a custom among the island red men, and one headland on the island is named Skull Point because of the many similar burials there. There is little doubt, however, owing to their proximity to the watch, coins and buttons, that the original six skeletons were of white men. The skulls were at first kept as souvenirs but have long since been lost or thrown away. One made a grisly workbench decoration for years, and others were kept at the lighthouse. Islander Web Steele recalls that fisherman Jim Van Every kept one on his tug the *Clara Mae,* until one day when Steele and Van Every were fishing for bass it rolled off the deck and was lost.

Of special importance is the fact that one skeleton was that of a man of large stature. Steele remembers another islander, Jim Doyle, who was fond of dramatizing the size of the jawbone by putting it completely over his own!

Could this be giant Luke, the ill-tempered Danish pilot?

Charlie Joyce, another old-timer on Manitoulin, remembers that some items that appeared to be cannon rammers were found among the wreckage and, like some of the skulls, were kept for a time at the lighthouse as curiosities.

A local fisherman once fouled his lines and drew to the

surface a large anchor. But before he could secure a stout line to it his tackle parted, and the anchor quickly plunged to the bottom. There is still another account of fishermen fouling their lines in what, when it was pulled near the surface, seemed to be a planked section of the wreck, with its lead caulking still in place. But here again the wreckage broke away to return to the bottom of Mississagi Strait.

Many interested individuals have investigated the site since the early 1900's, sincere people who sought only to determine if the wreck was actually that of the *Griffon*. The late Harry G. Tucker, a distinguished barrister from Owen Sound, first became familiar with the wreck when still a young man and in later years led an expedition to the site in search of additional relics. In 1931 Mr. C. H. J. Snider of Toronto, an authority on early ship-building and a marine author of some note, made an extensive survey of the wreck or what was left of it, hoping to arrive at some accurate measurements and to obtain a sampling of the ironwork for analysis. A report later issued by Mr. C. E. Plummer, technical director of chemical and metallurgical engineering of Chicago's Robert W. Hunt Company, indicated that the ironwork could well have been made by a process in use in northern Europe in the seventeenth century. Of the surviving timbers and planking Mr. Snider voiced the opinion that they were probably much too heavy for a craft such as the *Griffon* and bore no marks of the crude broadax or adze one might expect to find in ship timbers felled and hewn near the shipyard itself. The long bolts in the timbers had hand-filed threaded ends on which were wrought iron washers and large square threaded nuts.

Others who devoted much time in attempting to identify the wreck positively were the late Roy F. Fleming for the Toronto Department of Public Works and George Fox who conducted research for Commander Eugene F. McDonald of Chicago.

More recently two Cleveland, Ohio, men have spent their summers probing for more relics, studying all accounts given by the old-timers among the islanders, cataloging and documenting evidence previously found and tracking down items passed around as curios in years gone by. Both Frank A. Myers and Richard P. Tappenden have inspired interest and cooperation on the part of the residents, who have only recently become aware that the shores of their beloved island perhaps hold one of the great secrets of local history. Myers is honorary president of the Manitoulin Historical Society.

Convinced that there were still many undiscovered relics and bits of ironwork buried in the sand or awash near the wreck, Myers, in 1958, induced a party of Detroit skindivers to join him in a one-day expedition to the site. In only a few hours they recovered 165 pieces of ironwork in the form of bolts, washers, spikes, nuts and several samples of the original lead caulking. The divers found that the shore profile shelves off quickly, a depth of seventy feet being reached only a short distance from the beach. There are many accounts of fishermen tangling their lines and nets in wreckage in even deeper water in the strait, and Myers hopes soon to have the area scientifically combed by a vessel with underwater detection gear or the recently developed underwater television equipment. According to early records the stern of the ship was never fully above water, and it is thought to have slipped down into the deep water areas. There, too, perhaps, are the brass cannon the *Griffon* carried. The recovery of even one of these would be a major victory for the Manitoulin searchers. In 1942 a heavy storm washed a large section of the wreck back into deep water, and one can only surmise that after over two centuries of such storms there is much still to be brought to the surface.

Both wreck sites are well within the probable course of the *Griffon,* had she been driven eastward from the Straits of Mackinac in a gale. It is easy to imagine her piling up on the Manitoulin shore with her drenched and exhausted crew taking what shelter they could find in the crevices and caves in the rocky bluff, there to perish in the bitter cold the north country can produce in September. Indeed, since the Indians they might encounter could well be hostile, they had little choice!

Likewise, as the proponents of the Russell Island site maintain, the ship could have been overwhelmed and capsized in the storm, losing her cannon, equipment and cargo. The derelict hull could then very possibly have been carried among the hundreds of small islands of Georgian Bay to come to rest finally in shallow water where Orrie Vail's father first sighted her years ago. This would account for the jetsam the Indians had shown La Salle, the missing armament and the lack of other substantial relics.

The wreck itself, when Vail removed it to Tobermory for safekeeping, consisted only of a weathered old 12-inch-square keel marked by thirty-three notches. Still in place were the battered remains of her sternson and stemson, each apparently cut from natural crooks of trees. Still attached to the keel were a number of small "ribs" on the port side of the vessel. The entire starboard side was missing, and the keel, which measures about 40 feet, strongly suggests a ship about the size of the *Griffon.* In any event, nearly three hundred years of attrition by the elements left little else on which to base authoritative opinion.

A technologist in the Dominion Government Forest Products Laboratories, Mr. J. D. Hale, and Dr. A. D. Tushingham of the Royal Ontario Museum of Archaeology, after examining specimens of wood and iron from the wreck, both stated that they could very easily be three hundred years old.

Seeking to further verify his prize, Vail still plans a systematic search of the bottom of the lagoon in which the keel lay. There is the possibility that the storm-battered *Griffon*, driven far from her intended course, had anchored nearby to wait out further bad weather, only to have her anchors drag in a sudden shift of wind and to come crashing ashore on the rocks! Finding her anchors or, better yet, one or more of the seven cannon with the fleur-de-lis engraved upon the barrels would, as in the case of the Manitoulin wreck, solve the mystery.

La Salle was never fully satisfied that his ship had met her doom in a great storm, in spite of the wreckage cast up by the seas. It could not have come from another vessel for there was none! Still, he was haunted by the nagging suspicion of treachery on the part of Luke and his sailors. Indeed, from the position of the Russell Island hulk, it would appear that the ship had been beached with seamanlike proficiency which, in the season of high water, would have been relatively simple. From the complete lack of remains of the starboard side it is also possible to surmise that it had been deliberately destroyed, either by the crew or by fur pirates.

Several years after the *Griffon* vanished a young Indian told La Salle that shortly after the disappearance he had seen a white man being held prisoner by a tribe along the Mississippi River. He had been captured, so the Indian said, while making his way down the river by canoe in company with four other men, who were killed. From a description furnished by his informant, and other circumstances, La Salle concluded that the prisoner was none other than his pilot Luke the Dane!

The two camps of historians, each convinced that "their" wreck is the authentic one, have made energetic efforts to have their evidence substantiated by competent authorities. Unfortunately, even the experts disagree.

Rowley W. Murphy, well-known Canadian artist and illustrator, with sixty years of practical sailing experience himself, after having studied both wrecks and making detailed sketches of construction details of the Russell Island wreck, now favors it over the Manitoulin site.

In the absence of the original plans for the *Griffon*, Murphy points out that his deductions are based largely on the drawing of the ship that appeared in a book written by Hennepin. The friar did not make the drawing but, as Murphy points out, knew how to instruct the artist in depicting the correct lines and proportions. Admittedly, the artist used his license in the background where, quite incongruously, mountains and palm trees appear where none existed or are likely to exist. This artistic license, Murphy feels, did not apply to the dimensions and shape of the ship itself, which would have been done under the direction of Hennepin. Most important, he emphasizes, the length of the keel on the Russell Island hulk, and it was all there, would indicate a vessel such as the Hennepin book depicted.

When proponents of the Manitoulin site forwarded measurements and photographs of both wrecks to the Marine Museum of Paris, the subsequent comments and opinions of museum director T. Vichot and of M. Denoix, expert in naval archaeology, would seem to bear out their own claims.

The French authorities reported that from study of a survey made in 1672, they found that the French used iron bolts entirely in their ship bottoms whereas the English and Dutch used a great many wooden pegs. No wooden pegs were found in the Manitoulin wreck, but a number were recovered in the Russell Island hulk. The abundance of iron bolts such as distinguished the Manitoulin wreck was a characteristic definitely French before 1673, Vichot wrote, and for a long time afterward. Denoix was also of the opinion that the threaded bolts, in use since the time of the Romans, were probably more ancient than the type of ironwork in the other wreck. These were bolts with slots cut in them over which a washer was slipped and an iron wedge or key driven into the slot to make a quite effective fastening. The report from the museum also held that the dimensions of the timbers in the Manitoulin wreck were entirely possible for a ship with a keel of about fifty feet.

Those strongly in favor of the more recent discovery still maintain that the Manitoulin wreckage was that of a larger ship than the *Griffon* and emphasize that the lavish use of iron was not consistent with a ship built in the wilderness where every ounce of iron had to be shipped from Europe and carried overland many miles. This is contested on the basis that the builders were saltwater men. and would have built their vessel of the same structural strength as an ocean ship, particularly since they were to sail into entirely unknown waters!

In 1937 Commander McDonald and George Fox sent forty-nine specimens of wood to the University of Chicago for tree ring comparisons. The samples included some from the Manitoulin wreck, white oak stumps from the Niagara area dating within the seventeenth century and others from an old fort near the site of the *Griffon's* launching. The university's dendrochronologist, Dr. Florence Hawley, was unable to give a definite opinion, pointing out that there is not enough variation in rainfall near Buffalo to show significant variations in annual tree growth. The old method of dating wooden objects with radioactive carbon was not employed, since it has an accuracy variance of one hundred twenty years either way.

Excavations along the waterfront at Kingston, Ontario, in 1953 revealed the long buried hulks of old French ships. The timber structure, like that of the Manitoulin wreck, indicated massive frames with ribs spaced close together.

Very recently archaeologists have made extensive use of an improved radioactive carbon method of dating many objects. This is a complicated chemical process, done in a laboratory and using a special arrangement of Geiger counters. Further refinements of the method now permit the dating of old timbers with a plus or minus factor of only thirty years. Those qualified to perform the tests, however, are already occupied in extensive and continuing research projects. Both sides in the Tobermory–Manitoulin controversy have agreed to submit specimens when the technical process of determination can be scheduled.

Meanwhile, the search for more evidence goes on, and here, particularly in the Mississagi Strait off Manitoulin, exciting adventure waits for the *scuba* diver! Large sections of the ancient ship, possibly the vessel's stern, the researchers feel, are still in deep water offshore. The recovery of the stern, with perhaps the carved griffon still attached, would end the long dispute once and for all!

Such is the tale of the *Griffon*, a puzzling collection of evidence that is still inconclusive. Two wrecks and nothing more—two wrecks that lay neglected for centuries while the droppings of sea gulls whitened their bones and thoughtless hands tore them apart for their iron. How regrettable that relics that might today provide the final proof of the *Griffon's* fate have long since been put to the practical uses of fishing and farming only to have been lost, discarded or forgotten in time, even as the hulk from which they came.

Today the massive ore freighters keep well to the west of Manitoulin Island whether they swing westward through the Straits of Mackinac or set course for Detour passage and the Soo. Likewise, the steamers and ferryboats that ply the Georgian Bay ports give the island's headlands a wide berth. But on cold September nights, when the fog lies heavy over Lake Huron, their hoarse and mournful whistles carry over the waters to the caves where the sleeping skeletons lay hidden and to the beach where the wreck of their ship rested for nearly two centuries.

One wonders if the ghosts of the men who sailed her are listening?

# Bibliography

Associated Press     "Lake Huron Treasure Hunt," November, 1951.

Ballin, Fred A.     "Bessemer Steel in Shipbuilding," *Marine Review*, 1893.

Bodsworth, Fred     "They're Looting Our History," *Maclean's Magazine*, November 1, 1952.

*The Bulletin*     "Shoal Searchers," *The Bulletin*, Lake Carriers' Association; November, 1951.

Boyer, Dwight     "Lost at Sea," *Toledo Blade*, November 25, 1951.

Boyer, Dwight     "Open Water Ahead," *Steelways*, March, 1958.

*Cleveland Plain Dealer*     "Bramley Expedition," April 6, 1930.

Dosey, Herbert W.     "City of Erie–Tashmoo Race," *The Bulletin*, November, 1958.

Ericson, Bernard E.     "First Real Ships to Sail Our Lakes Were La Salle's Sloops," *The Bulletin*, October, 1953.

Fleming, Roy F.     "First Sailor of the Upper Lakes," *The Canadian*, August, 1929.

*Great Lakes Shipping*     Lake Carriers' Association.

Green, J. B.     *Diving With and Without Armor!*, Faxon's Steam Power Press, Buffalo, New York, 1859.

Hane, Wil     *Lorain Journal*, November 28, 1958.

Laidly, W. T.

"The United States Lake Survey Steamer *Peary.*" U.S. Army Engineer District, March, 1961.

*Long Beach California Press-Telegram*

January 30, 1930. "Mayan Explorers Made Honorary Members of Club of Adventurers."

Mansfield, J. B.

*History of the Great Lakes,* J. H. Beers and Co., Chicago, 1899.

Martin, W. P.

"Canadian Registry Record of Steamship *Peary,*" National Revenue, Canada, Halifax, N.S.

*Marine Review*

"Sworn Statement of H. W. Stewart." Issues of September 3 and 8, 1892.

McLean, John

"Lost *Griffon* Thought Found," *The Toronto Telegram,* August 16, 17, 1955.

Murphy, Rowley W.

"Discovery of the Wreckage of the *Griffon,*" *Inland Seas,* The Great Lakes Historical Society, Spring, 1956.

Myers, Frank A.

"Recollections of the Manitoulin Wreck," *The Recorder,* Gore Bay, Ontario, May 13, 1954.

*Newsweek*

"Copper Treasure Hunt," September 1, 1952.

Plummer, C. E.

Technical Director, Robert W. Hunt Company, Chicago. (Report on analyzing iron bars from Manitoulin wreck.) 1931.

*Register of American Yachts*

Lloyd's, New York, N.Y., 1923–1932.

Remick, Teddy

Great Lakes Shipwreck Listings, Cleveland, Ohio, 1965.

Snider, C. H. J.

"Further Search for the *Griffon,*" *Ontario History,* January, 1952.

Snider, Jack

"Lake Superior Has Taken Many Vessels and Lives to the Bottom," *Fort William Daily Times-Journal,* June 22, 1962.

Spavin, Don

"Does Lake Superior Still Contain a Fortune in Silver?" *St. Paul Sunday Pioneer-Press,* September 19, 1965.

Scott, Beryl H.

"Silver Islet Landing," *Canadian Geographical Journal,* March, 1956.

Scott, Beryl H.

"The Story of Silver Islet," *Ontario History,* Vol. XLIX No. 3.

Tappenden, Richard P.

"A Possible Solution to the Mystery of the *Griffon,*" *Inland Seas,* Winter, 1946.

Williams, Edward T.  "The Inter-Continental Romance of the *Griffon*," *Niagara Falls (NY) Gazette*, September 28, 1938.

Williams, Elmer  "Lake Erie Tragedies," *Toledo Blade*, June 30, 1930.

# Index